Also by the Author

This Mystery and I

The Little Book of Awareness

The Quiet Place Within

Talks With Temerlen

Transforming Negative Emotions

The Heart of Awareness

author@pantheonprosebooks.com

The Place of Precious Things

PETER INGLE

The Place of Precious Things

Copyright © 2023 by Peter Ingle

All Rights Reserved

Produced in the United States of America

First edition 2023

No part of this publication may be reproduced, store, or transmitted, in any form, or by any means, electronic, mechanical, photocopying, recording, or otherwise, without permission in writing from the author.

Library of Congress Cataloging-in-Publication Data

Ingle, Peter M.
The Place of Precious Things

ISBN: 978-1-7367425-3-2

pantheonprosebooks.com

cover design by Olivia Ingle
cover image by Harry Cooke

Foreword

The expression 'Pure Being' throughout this dialogue refers to the conscious source of being that is *behind* awareness. By way of analogy, although we say the sun shines on the earth, it is actually the sun's manifestation *as* light which enlivens the earth. The source of that light remains as the source even as it extends itself in the *form* of light. It is also true that light is an inevitable part of the heat generated by the sun, so the two are in a sense one. Nevertheless, light cannot assume to be, or to fully know, the sun. Only the sun contains recognition of itself as the source of light *and* as the manifestation of light.

This distinction brings clarity to the idea of being aware of being aware, which is akin to light knowing itself, while beyond that there is a pureness of being that encompasses even the deepest point of awareness. This inexplicable pureness is the same *being* that the ninth-century Zen master Huang Po called 'Pure Mind' and 'The Place of Precious Things'.

In trying to describe the 'recognition' of Pure Being, words inevitably get in the way, yet words can explain *to the mind* what Pure Being is *not*. In doing so, words can open a door into the vastness of Pure Being beyond the mind and beyond awareness.

One purpose of this dialogue is to highlight what Pure Being is *not* by describing the illusory nature of what we experience as 'I' and 'me'. This sense of self stems from the psychological formation of an ego which regards the mind as 'my' mind and the body as 'my' body, and then extends that view to include 'my' thoughts, 'my' life, 'my' experiences, 'my' needs and wants, and 'my' suffering—all of which are tied to a *mental image of self.* When this image is seen as just a projection of the mind, this 'reveals' the reality of Pure Being which recognizes that it is always above, below, and around the projection of 'me' even though it had fallen sway to believing the projection was real and that it *was* the projection.

Another purpose of this dialogue is to explain the physiological and psychological basis on which the feeling of identity is built, why it *appears to be* real, how it perpetuates itself in the psyche, and how perceiving it can lead to the recognition of Pure Being *at its source.*

CONTENTS

Mind and Ego 1

Negative Emotions 29

The Psychology of the Ego 79

Essence and Personality 105

Life on Earth 125

Human Suffering 139

Spiritual Teachers 153

Pure Being 161

The Place of Precious Things is a place to which no directions can be given. All we can say is that it is close by. It cannot be exactly described, but when you have a tacit understanding of its substance, it is there.

Huang Po

Mind and Ego

The Place of Precious Things

Man has closed himself up, till he sees all things
through narrow chinks of his cavern.

William Blake

You say that Pure Being is just another name for what Huang Po called Pure Mind. Why the difference?

He used capital letters. He said 'Pure Mind' to imply something more than and beyond the intellect and emotions. I call it Pure Being to make clear that it has nothing to do with the ordinary mind. Pure Being is a void that recognizes thoughts as material spawned in the mind, but it is usually identified with the mind and takes itself to be the mind having thoughts. Identification means that Pure Being, unaware of itself, takes up residence in the mind *as the self* having thoughts.

We are so used to thoughts that we presume they are 'me'. Yet something can perceive this feeling of 'me' behind thoughts. That something is Pure Being. All it needs to do (although 'do' is not the best word) is realize that it is seeing 'me' and 'my' thoughts within the void of itself.

The fact that the mind projects thoughts inside itself is astonishing. More astonishing is that you can see thoughts inside the mind, see your sense of self having them, *and* be aware of both. Recognizing this brings you beyond the mind to the threshold of the void of Pure Being.

Does Pure Being control the mind from behind the scenes?

The mind wants to control the mind, just as the body wants to control the body. Both are dominated by a sense of identity in the ego. Pure Being is not interested in controlling any of them because it is not inherently attached to them. They are all *forms* of energy. It is not. It is their source. It is simply the pure energy of the void of being. But when it identifies it *takes form* as a feeling of self in the mind and body. Every few seconds, this feeling reestablishes itself as a sense of 'I' in the mind which provides a reference point of psychological security, stability, and identity. Without this reference point there is simply the emptiness of being. But the ego fills this emptiness by clinging to a central form of identity as a person.

The ego is an image that forms in the mind as a feeling of 'I'. Most people spend their entire life immersed in the mirage of this feeling of identity. Their Pure Being is attached to a psychological hologram that is producing images about itself in the form of thoughts and emotions. The hologram cannot see that it is a hologram, but Pure Being can see it and when it recognizes this, it recognizes itself as the void in which the hologram appears. But a hologram cannot appear in a void, so when this recognition occurs the hologram vanishes. It gets absorbed by the void.

So Pure Being is the awareness of thoughts?

Thoughts are one thing. The mind is another. Awareness of both is another. And the void out of which *all of these* manifest is yet another. The mind cannot think or feel its way to this void of Pure Being. At some point during the spiritual 'search' the ladder of thought comes to its end and the void recognizes itself as the void.

From this perspective, it is interesting to consider what the mind is as a psychological *structure*. For example, what comprises an empty versus a full mind? What is the mind without thoughts? What are thoughts? How do they function in the mind? What do they have to do with the sense of self? What lies beyond the sense of self? Few people in history have penetrated the reality behind these questions.

What is happening when I try to stop thoughts or control them? For example, if I want to redirect them to another subject?

If you try to stop thoughts, you will notice that the mind is trying to stop its own thoughts. So stopping thought is not the way out of the mind because that effort is taking place in the mind. The way out is to notice that the feeling of 'me' noticing the mind and the feeling of the mind controlling or redirecting itself are all happening *in the void of being.*

Instead of trying to stop thoughts, the awareness of being can extract itself from the stream of thought. When this awareness focuses *itself*, it sees the mind turning and knows intuitively not to get caught in the web of identification with thoughts.

Some people practice a technique of watching to see the next thought arise. Is this also the mind?

It can be, especially if it is a technique. Another technique is to keep noticing that you are watching. Instead of worrying about thoughts, which is what the ego would like you to do, keep steering the mind toward awareness and steering awareness toward Pure Being. Just simple being behind awareness recognizing all that is going on. When you first start noticing your inner world, it looks like everything is packed together. All the thoughts, emotions, and sensations feel squeezed into a small space. Consequently, it is easy to be identified with *what* you see instead of being aware of *seeing* and recognizing the *being* of seeing. The more you notice and the more you realize you are noticing, the more the space opens up between everything. Pure Being becomes more free as the spaciousness of inner space.

You mentioned that Pure Being is the source of all these life forms. Can you say more how this works?

The four centers of the mind and body by themselves have no identity. For that they need the injection of a life force that comes in the form of the rarefied substance of Pure Being. With this energy, human beings can interact psychologically with other human beings. At the same time, this substance—this 'being'—in everyone is capable of recognizing *itself*, although it does not begin the human journey this way. It begins it unconsciously, and because it is unconscious, it sticks to the mind, and the more it sticks the more it forms as a parasite of identity that enables the mind to experience itself as 'me' and 'my' body.

What about when I use attention to steer my thoughts and hold them in a certain direction?

All four centers of the mind and body can operate with attention, but there is an important difference between attention and awareness. If you observe closely you will see that attention is a 'tension' of the 'extension' of awareness as it 'goes out' to encounter all the forms of creation. Meanwhile, the source of that awareness—the void of Pure Being—is always at home, even when it sends the attention of awareness on an errand.

We are so accustomed to thoughts and emotions that we never question what they are as forms of energy that manifest psychologically. We also overlook the fact that we can see them. Instead, we identify with them and take them to be our being. We grant them authenticity as identity and give them permission to lead us through life at the expense of Pure Being recognizing the void of itself—which is more than a void but which, compared to the somethingness of the mind and body, is empty nothingness.

Pure Being is not a function of the mind. It has nothing to do with the mind except when it attaches to, identifies with, and appropriates thoughts and emotions in the form of 'I's. But even then it is not a function of the mind. It is simply caught up in the mind by all the 'I's produced in the mind, and caught up in the sense of ego created by identification.

So I should give up trying to control my attention?

Controlling your attention is a good thing, a useful thing. It is simply that there is more beyond that. For example, in addition to focusing on thoughts themselves, it is possible to focus on being aware of the *structure* of the mind that produces thoughts. This structure is quiet. It is just a container that fills with thoughts. All it is doing is reflecting impulses that surface within it. When you see this, the operation of the mind changes. Thoughts cease to feel personal. You start to see them as objects in the mind, and the structure of the mind starts to resonate with the emptiness of the void of being. And this is true even when you are controlling thoughts.

Whether you trace a thought or emotion to its origin, or follow it to it's conclusion, they both lead to the same thing. You can also turn away from the feeling of 'I' in all thoughts and emotions and simply keep looking for being *as being*.

The same thing applies to the body. Instead of focusing on movements and postures, it is possible to be aware of how the underlying structure of the body is inherently still. Whereas the mind is a silent mirror that reflects thought and emotion, the body is a platform of stillness from which sensation and movement arise. This stillness also resonates with the emptiness of the void of being.

Do the mind and body perceive on their own?

Yes, although they both have restricted fields of perception that are not aware beyond the scope of their immediate needs and existence. For example, the body does not see much farther than the next meal or job or home or mate. And the mind does not see much farther than its sense of a person with preferences and opinions.

In both cases, the mystery of existence and being able to notice existence goes *unrecognized*.

At the same time, however, the body and mind are transformers in their own right. The body takes in a certain kind of food that it chews, swallows, digests, disperses as energy, and eliminates. The mind does the same thing. It takes in visual and audio impressions of the world as types of food that it chews, swallows, digests, disperses as thought and emotion, and eliminates. But the mind is more sophisticated as a transformer. Where the body uses its food for subsistence, the mind uses visual and audio impressions to interpret its relationship to the environment. Animals do this with their instinctive and moving centers, but humans do it with the additional faculties of thought and emotion which enable the ego to coagulate and distinguish itself as separate and unique.

The body cannot transform energy in the mind, and the mind cannot transform energy in the body, but Pure Being is the ultimate transformer. It can transform the energy in both the body and the mind as well as in itself. The 'food' that Pure Being eats, how it digests that food, and the nature of what it eliminates are all of a different order of dimension than those of the body and mind.

Pure Being is outside 'me', outside the stream

of thoughts, outside the cycle of emotions, and outside the feeling of 'I' having thoughts and emotions. If it were not outside all of these, we would not be seeing them.

At the same time, Pure Being in most people is stuck inside the mind as a sense of 'I'. This is true even as you learn about spirituality and try to awaken. Without knowing it, you are trying to awaken from *inside* the sense of 'I' whereas Pure Being resides beyond that. This is easy to see from beyond the mind, hard to understand from inside it. But that is why we talk about it. Talking about it helps shift the view.

I have trouble seeing the difference between my mind and my thoughts. How do you see the difference?

The mind is a theater in the brain where you can see images of thought, emotion, and sensation appear each moment on center stage and act themselves out in the name of 'I'. The innocence of Pure Being normally sits in the front row of the theater with its chin on the stage convinced that it is seeing itself on stage. When it realizes what is going on, it sits up, then it moves to the back row, then it sees it has the option of leaving the theater as well as leaving the neighborhood, the city, the country, the planet, and the solar system. At a certain point, the theater, the drama, and the main character have no more interest and hold no more pull. They vanish in the distance.

But even when Pure Being perceives that it can see thoughts in the mind, the mind will take hold of this perception and experience itself as a patron sitting in the theater. At that point, Pure Being is less identified with the action on stage but it is still identified with the feeling of 'I' watching the mind. Sometimes it becomes aware of the mind *and* the feeling of 'I' viewing the mind and recognizes it is neither. It keeps backing farther and farther away from *what* it perceives.

Is this difference the same for all four centers?

The body and mind are like a house. The body is downstairs. The mind is upstairs. In fourth way parlance, downstairs includes the basement of the instinctive center and the first floor of the moving center. Above that is the second floor of the emotional center and the third floor of the intellectual center. Pure Being is the empty space inside the house and surrounding the house. It is also the entire house. It is all of it and none of it. It is everything and nothing *at the same time*, which sounds preposterous to the mind but is nevertheless true from the perspective of Pure Being.

You can also envision your 'house' with hundreds of doors, each opening into a different group of sensations, movements, thoughts, and feelings. Identification happens when Pure Being takes interest in a door, then ventures inside and attaches itself to whatever is inside. It 'forgets' itself as Pure Being and experiences itself as a sense of 'I' in the room it enters.

Even as Pure Being stands on the threshold of one of the four centers, it is already assimilating itself as a sense of 'I'. It is *forming itself into* 'I' am 'my' thoughts, 'my' feelings, 'my' sensations. When it retires to the spaciousness of itself and 'remembers itself' as Pure Being, the sense of 'I' falls away. There is just the recognition of formless being. Sensations, thoughts, and emotions are no longer imbued with a sense of self. As a result, they take on a neutral hue as objects.

Where is Pure Being in relation to the mind?

Pure Being 'pops' out of the mind. It is already out, but it's hooks are in the mind. It has to unbend its hooks, as Nisargadatta said. When it does, it pops back into the wholeness of itself as Pure Being.

Pure Being also does not think. It is not about thought. It is Pure Being whose home ground is the recognition of everything *being* now. It does not need thought and does not need to rely on thought to *be* this recognition and to realize that it both includes thoughts *and* is free of thoughts when it is not identified.

When Pure Being finds itself identified with thought, it can choose to be not identified. Poof. Not identified. But something in us does not want it to be that easy. That something *wants* to cling to the hope that *it* will be free. This wanting and hoping and the feeling of identity behind them become a main hindrance to Pure Being recognizing itself.

After all the words have been said and all the concepts explained, Pure Being has to intuit how to let go of identification with thoughts, and let go of being the letter go of thoughts, and keep drifting away as spacious void.

So it is not even a peaceful mind?

Peace cannot be found in the mind. You have to see the futility of that, the reality of that. The troubles you feel are the result of your mind's way of thinking about them which in turn is the result of you *imagining yourself as a self* who is a justice seeker and rule enforcer and entitled person who knows what is right and wrong, what should be done, why you deserve better, and so on. None of that is Pure Being. It is all a projection of the ego. What needs to be dissolved and resolved is identification with the sense of 'I' who has issues. The peace you want is just beyond. Just a hairsbreadth beyond.

Does the struggle for inner peace feel like a struggle because it is in fact the mind struggling?

Yes. The body and mind renounce, resist, deny, struggle, and force. Pure Being does none of these things. Nor does it regard itself as 'I'. It sees thoughts and emotions and pain and joy, and sees 'I' struggling with them, and it lets all of these simply be without interfering. That is how it transcends them.

Even attitudes of acceptance and positive thinking have limits because they are simply one part of the mind counterbalancing resistance in another part of the mind. Even if the result is a neutral mind, it is all happening in the mind. It is not a conscious transformation of Pure Being.

I get the vicious circle you are describing, but it is hard to step all the way out, partly because the thoughts just keep coming.

Yes, they keep coming, keep spinning. But they change when we change our relationship to them because they are just projections. Thoughts—and emotions—feel real only because we believe them. When we believe them, they take flight. Without the support of our belief they cannot fly. They are also not the 'problem'. The problem is that we believe the sense of self having thoughts. The thoughts and our mental image of self then reinforce one another. But the true Self, which is not a self, is neither. It is the void of spacious being in which the images of thoughts and the idea of self *appear*.

Even when we see a thought, it still has to run its course. Pure Being simply ceases to run with it. The same is true of our life which in many ways is itself a thought in a bigger context. But when this is recognized, the thought of our life still has to run its course. Nevertheless, stepping beyond the mind is a challenge because we are so accustomed to seeing and digesting everything with the mind. We don't know how to perceive without concepts, labels, interpretations, judgments, conclusions, and so on.

Realizing that you are seeing thoughts and not granting them legitimacy as a sense of 'I' boosts the recognition of Pure Being. It is like rising from the earth, seeing it from space, and realizing you *are* space. If you fall back to earth you just have to keep boosting yourself into being by observing thoughts and realizing you are observing them. At a certain point Pure Being keeps floating in space.

Part of the reason I find it difficult to step out of the mind is because things start to feel vague and helpless.

That is true for the mind, and particularly for the ego established in the mind. But it is not true for Pure Being. The problem is that we think the mind needs to do all the work all the time, but this is not true. The mind is not needed as an instrument of perception. It is meant to be a mental filter for sifting perceptions, not for becoming them. But it is so used to occupying the first position that it has become greedy about grasping and assessing and concluding at every turn. And the ego has come to rely on this mental activity for security. This is why Pure Being needs to see, not just thoughts, but the feeling of 'I' behind them to reach a full recognition of itself as the void. Otherwise it remains stuck in the thought of 'I' am trying to see 'my' thoughts and not be them.

But is the mind really capable of coming round to this understanding and stepping out of itself?

Paradoxically, Pure Being uses the mind as a lever to look for Pure Being so that Pure Being will recognize itself looking. The mind, by itself, never does anything. To the mind it feels as though 'I' will eventually break out of the mind and be free, but in reality what happens is that Pure Being recognizes itself *already* outside the mind and this unplugs the illusion of 'I' which then fizzles. Much of our difficulty is that we are trying to approach all of this *from the inside*.

What about spiritual practices?

Spiritual 'practices' are the mind trying to render Pure Being tangible according to the mind's idea of what Pure Being is. This is all the mind revolving inside itself which is why it can sometimes make you feel stuck, because you *are* stuck in the mind. It is also the mind that produces the thought, "I should probably just stop doing these practices." Even with that thought you remain stuck in the mind believing there is a problem. And there *is* a problem until you realize you are seeing it as Pure Being.

Meditation, for instance, is not a way *of* Pure Being. It is a mental approach *to* being. It is the mind preparing the way. Meditation is intended to align your psychological 'now' with your physical 'now' in the present 'now' so as to enable Pure Being to recognize itself above and below and around 'you' meditating. Meditation can also be seen as scaffolding assembled by the intellectual center. At its best, this scaffolding tries to get out of its own way to allow for the void and defer to the void. Yoga is a similar form of scaffolding assembled by the moving center, as is prayer in the emotional center. All of them can become an end in themselves *or* serve as platforms of entry into the void of being.

In my experience, meditation invites awareness whether I am wound up or already calm.

Meditation can create a conducive atmosphere for Pure Being, but Pure Being does not meditate. It does not get wound up and does not calm down. When it identifies, though, this causes the four centers to react. They are the ones who get wound up. But you cannot sit and meditate each time you get wound up, and calming down afterwards doesn't help if you keep getting wound up again. You want to find the cure at its source which is Pure Being, and this is not reserved for periods of meditation. It is always in relation to what is happening now.

Try to discern in yourself the difference between meditating and conscious being. One is in the mind. The other is not. One thinks about meditating. The other does not. One meditates while the other sees 'you' meditating.

But the mind seems capable of understanding this. It is discussing it right now.

The mind itself cannot know the truth of Pure Being, even though this is where the search seems to begin. The mind thinks it is a sufficient starting point and that it can carry on all the way to the destination and discover Pure Being for itself. But it is not so. Pure Being can begin and arrive only at itself.

The mind knows very little about Pure Being. The best it can do is interpret perceptions that reflect onto it from the awareness being emitted from Pure Being. The mind is all talk. Pure Being is all being. This does not change even as the mind becomes sophisticated with its talk about awakening, enlightenment, and so on. Pure Being uses the mind to search for itself. Then the mind gets in the way and confuses the search. Then Pure Being has to recognize itself. Once it does, it still uses the mind to transpose perceptions through the mind. It is a kind of cosmic dance with Pure Being always leading even when the mind thinks it is leading.

Doesn't the mind conceive or perceive that it is searching for the truth?

It does, but only on the level of itself, in the dimension of the mind. We start the quest for Pure Being from a position that feels like 'I' am trying to awaken, that 'I' want to be enlightened, that 'I' am searching for myself. Then at some point Pure Being realizes it can see 'I' doing all that and thinking all that and presuming to be real. All of that resides as identity in the mind, whereas Pure Being has no identity.

The mind is also convinced that there is a mental ladder it can climb step by step to reach Pure Being, which the mind envisions as a thing, an accomplishment, a more developed version of itself. Fortunately this is impossible because if it was possible we would settle for that instead of the real thing. But the mind is not doing this on purpose. It is not trying to get in the way or get out of the way. It is just operating as the mind. Pure Being sees the mind, steps out of the mind, and recognizes the infinite void that it is.

The mistake we make with the mind is to regard it as a source of perception when the truth is that the mind does not perceive as such. Pure Being perceives what is happening as it happens, while the mind interprets what was perceived *after* it happens. The ego then uses the mind's interpretations to reference everything back to itself. This is what 'I' think. This is 'my' conclusion, 'my' opinion, and 'my' reasoning. In short, the mind ceases to be just a filtering mechanism and becomes an extension of the ego which the ego uses to project and protect and justify itself.

When the mind is stuck in a loop of thoughts

and cannot get out it is because Pure Being is identified with the mind, and this identification is causing the mind to struggle against itself. But Pure Being doesn't realize this when it is identified. It presumes to be the mind thinking, "I cannot stop these thoughts." But this is just the mind turning on itself.

If you strip the ego out of the mind, you are left with a mind that is capable of producing thoughts and feelings but without the need to reference all of them back to itself and deduce a sense of identity from them. The mind then becomes a pure vessel for thought. Its engine runs more smoothly, quietly, and efficiently.

But can the mind really function without an identity?

Oh, yes. We are not born with a sense of identity. It accumulates in the mind through repeated bursts of identification that form the ego. The habit of identification is like an intravenous device inserted into our psychology. Once it is in, any drug can be infused at any time. Any thought, sensation, or emotion becomes available as an experience and confirmation of 'I'.

Our sense of identity is not just randomly formed when we get identified, is it?

Our sense of identity is formed by the multiple factors of culture, race, religion, education, language, social customs, and more, but when you peel away all those layers you find the same underlying ingredient of identity in everyone; the same core feeling of 'I'. This is no accident because the base sense of identity in each of us derives from the same source of Pure Being that gets attached to all these bodies and minds. But Pure Being cannot be explained to the mind because the mind is just an organ. At best, this organ transposes reflections of awareness into thought. But we are so accustomed to thoughts and to thinking of ourselves as our thoughts that it takes time for Pure Being to recognize itself beyond perception and beyond the feeling of being a unique person.

And a unique person with unique problems…

Yes. Before we can have a 'problem' we have to have an identity and we have to believe in it. We have to take it seriously. Then it takes the problem seriously. What seem like 'my' problems stem from our sense of identity and its *relationship to* the world. This sense of identity stems from identification, and identification stems from the unrecognition (the unconsciousness) of Pure Being.

When you glimpse the feeling of 'I' in its entirety—as an image of your entire person—it will seem as though you are standing next to yourself looking at a human being and seeing it *imagining itself* as the identity of a person who has thoughts about having problems. Another way to say it is that Pure Being can see perceptions funneling through the mind as reflections that take form as thoughts, and that when it identifies with thoughts it *becomes* the ego.

So self-preoccupation creates the self?

It perpetuates it. There is always an astonishing world right in front of us that we don't notice because we are preoccupied as an identity in the mind. You see this in people walking down the street. They barely see the sidewalk because awareness is buried in thoughts inside the mind, or immersed in the digital screen in their hands. The wonder of creation and the double wonder of being a witness of creation both go unnoticed. In this sense, our head is like a pair of binoculars. Ordinarily when we look through binoculars we focus on objects in the distance. We forget that our head is behind the binoculars, that our eyes are seeing through the lens, and that we are behind our eyes looking *through* them. Most people think they are the binoculars and that their life is what is being seen in the distance. The innocence of Pure Being remains unrecognized *right here* behind these binoculars we call eyes.

Sometimes I realize this and start to see the world differently, but then self-preoccupation takes over again. Is this how it usually works?

If the ego manages to hide for a time, as soon as the occasion permits it will storm back and do its usual dance. Yes, this is normal and can even be useful because the contrast of the ego having been away and then returning makes it very obvious, which in turn makes the realization that you are seeing it also very obvious, and this realization can open the door for the recognition of Pure Being.

I find that thinking about god is a good antidote to self-preoccupation.

The limits of the mind and the hubris of the ego are evident in the presumption that we as a person can understand god simply by forming an image or intuiting a notion about what god is *as an entity*. But the mind cannot 'think' god. Whatever it thinks is limited to a mental concept. Pure Being, however, can recognize the infinite depths *of itself*. This recognition is not physical or emotional or psychological or intuitive. It is the profound reality of the conscious void of Pure Being which is the source of everything.

~ ~ ~

Negative Emotions

The Place of Precious Things

I wish I could show you
when you are lonely or in darkness
the astonishing light of your own being.

Hafiz

Why are we so inclined to perceive things through the lens of negative emotions?

Negative emotions are not perceptions. They are *reactions* to perception. Awareness perceives and then the ego forms in layers of reaction to what is perceived. There is a perception, then a *physio*logical reaction, then a *psycho*logical response to the reaction—all in conjunction with our sense of 'I'. It happens so fast that we don't notice it, but the awareness of Pure Being can see all this and not get snared by it.

The mind and body form a circuit in which negative emotions become a current that passes through the circuit as a feeling of 'I' am irritated, 'I' am offended, 'I' am angry, "I' am hurt. We usually feel good about our negative emotions because they bring a surge of energy that fortifies our sense of 'I'.

Is the non-expression of negative emotions related to controlling this surge?

The tactic of not expressing negative emotions outwardly comes from the fourth way system. And yes, this 'non-expression' is about containing the surge of negative emotions in the sense of containing the energy *behind* them to make it available for transformation. Once that energy is discharged, this opportunity is lost. Not expressing negative emotions is a way of putting the brakes on their momentum to keep them from combusting. It is not about denying or suppressing or deflecting negative emotions. It is about freeing the energy behind them.

Why is the energy of the reaction negative to begin with?

The English word for 'negative' comes from the Latin word *negare* which means to negate or deny. That is what negative emptions do; they deny reality by negating the truth of how things really are—including how the ego is just a projection of the mind. But by denying reality the ego affirms itself. And the instinctive center helps it do exactly that because almost every human reaction starts as an impulse in the instinctive center which gets filtered by a sense of 'me' in the emotional and intellectual centers. The more negatively charged a reaction is, the more easily it becomes a negative emotion and the more intensely it gets tied to our feeling of 'I'.

The idea of transforming negative emotions means transcending both the emotional and the instinctive feeling of 'I' behind negative emotions. Transcending means Pure Being 'returning' to seeing things as they are without the identity of an ego needing to protect itself with a reactionary response.

Do negative emotions serve as ballast for the ego?

Negative emotions serve as containers for a particular kind of energy that is highly combustible in the atmosphere of identification. Within less than a second the ego can ignite this energy and use it to inflate itself with a sense of 'I' ranging from frustration, irritability, and anger to self-pity, resentment, and depression. Human beings are the only life form on earth—perhaps in the solar system and galaxy—capable of manufacturing this kind of energy and channeling it through the psychological form of an ego.

Transformation means harnessing negative emotions as leverage by not expressing them and thereby gaining access to their energy and passing it to the void of Pure Being where it can be absorbed by *and* expanded into the void. This energy normally reinforces the human ego, but it can instead engender the conscious recognition of Pure Being.

Negative emotions are part of the human psyche for a reason. It is no accident that this energy in humans provides the perfect combustible material for transformation. Negative emotions have a specific purpose both when they get expressed and when they get transformed. Most of the time, however, they are being indulged in by most of humanity which as a whole is an unwitting instrument for the unconscious discharge of this volatile energy.

So they are more like fuel than like ballast?

Yes. They are also reflections of the ego. Although they start as sensations in the instinctive center, this energy gets consolidated in the emotional and intellectual centers and then wrapped like sausage in the skin of the ego. The ego cannot exist for long without negative emotions because without them it has no air to breathe.

Each person's preferred negative emotions and preferred negative moods can also be seen as psychological addictions that have their root in the instinctive center. The impulse toward negativity always starts there and then seeps into the mind as emotional distress. When negative emotions arise inwardly and you express them outwardly, ask yourself who it is that is feeling negative and expressing the negativity. Ask yourself if that is the most pure part of your being. Ask yourself if you want to keep carrying on like that for the rest of your life or whether there is an alternative. What if this energy could be redirected and converted into a very different form for a very different purpose?

Isn't it the pain body who is negative?

You can think of what Eckhart Tolle calls the 'pain body' as the psychological apparatus where negative emotions are manufactured, indulged in, and expressed. Another name for the pain body is imaginary 'I'. It is the sense of self you imagine yourself to be, and it has its deepest roots in negative emotions because the energy behind them has contracted and become embedded as mechanisms of psychological defense.

Imaginary 'I' wants to bear the weight of everything that has gone wrong in the past and may possibly go wrong in the future because that weight gives it substance and significance. In doing so, it squeezes the recognition of Pure Being out of the picture. And this is the key thing to grasp: that imaginary 'I' behind negative emotions exists *at the expense of* Pure Being.

This is also why not expressing negative emotions is so pivotal because it can put the brakes on the psychological momentum of negativity long enough to free the energy that is fueling the notion of 'I'. That freed energy can then recirculate and transmute as Pure Being.

Why are negative emotions such a good candidate for transformation?

Because they mask the ego which we mistake as our real identity. But the truth is that *everything* can be transformed into the void of Pure Being. Everything you perceive, everything you think, everything you feel emotionally, everything you suffer, everything that you see suffering. They are all material for the awareness of Pure Being. But not all of them have the same catalytic power.

For example, negative emotions contain more combustible energy than thoughts, while suffering contains more energy than negative emotions. This is because real suffering (as opposed to psychologically manufactured suffering) is connected to our *essence* as a human being. Real suffering takes a heavy toll on essence, but in doing so it cleanses and purifies essence in a way that gives Pure Being the possibility of transcending identification with our *whole* person as a human being.

Ouspensky said two conscious 'shocks' are needed to achieve full transformation and that transformation needs to be preceded by self-remembering. How do you understand this?

Self-remembering refers to Pure Being recognizing itself as the void of being. Transformation means Pure Being then extracting the energy *behind* negative emotions, absorbing that energy, and resolving it in the void of itself. Whereas identification causes the 'substance' of being to congeal as 'I', non-identification allows that substance to release its *energy* back into its source in the void of Pure Being.

The word 'shock' in the fourth way is meant to imply the force of an influence coming from outside a process so the process can turn in a new direction or keep going in its original direction after having lost enough of its own energy to continue. Conscious shocks come from the conscious awareness of Pure Being, whereas mechanical shocks occur as automatic reactions in the mind and body.

The two conscious shocks of self-remembering and transformation are distinct yet connected. They are the same light, but the light has to turn on before it can shine. The two shocks also depend on each other and reinforce each other in the sense that a light cannot shine until it turns on, and it cannot keep shining unless it stays on. You will know when the light of awareness of Pure Being turns on and you will realize that it has to stay on if you want to transform negative emotions and transform suffering.

I assume you consider judgment to be a negative emotion. If so, why is it so incessant?

Judgment seems innocuous, but it is an invasive negative emotion that is incessant because of what lies behind it, which is the impulse to blame. We blame ourselves (as identities), others (as real people), circumstances (as something we control), the weather (ridiculous), and god (a mental fabrication).

The impulse to judge exists as the first and last defense of the ego. It never goes away until the ego is exposed. When that happens, there is no more 'you' and no more judgment. There is just the utter consciousness of things as they are.

If you know how to step around and through judgment, you can see things as they are. But this means transcending the ego. And only Pure Being can do that. Perception without judgment is very sobering because you no longer fool yourself about yourself, other people, the world, and your distorted opinion about all of them.

A judge rules on the law and dispenses punishment accordingly. This is what the ego does when it judges. It psychologically punishes others by limiting them to *its* idea of them as a person according to *its* idea of itself as a person. Ironically, judgment is more than a reflection of the judge; it is also a form of self-limitation and self-punishment. When we judge others, for example, we think we are punishing *them*, but we are actually putting *ourselves* in the prison of judgment. One of the strangest ways we punish others (their ego) is by putting ourselves (our ego) in the isolated confinement of ignoring them. We think we are isolating them when in fact we are isolating ourselves by confining ourselves (the ego) to its illusion of being uniquely better or uniquely worse than others.

Is everyone equally prone to judging?

It may seem that some people are less prone to judging because certain forms of judgment are not as obvious as others. But everyone swims in the sea of judgment. You could almost call it the psychological sea of humanity. Imagine if no one swam in this sea? What if everyone decided, "you know what, let's get out of this psychological cesspool and just have a party together on the beach." But, that's not going to happen anytime soon because it would mean everyone seeing the ego for what it is.

Because judgment is so pervasive, however, it can be one of the best foils against which to see your imaginary idea of yourself and see how entrenched the feeling of 'me' is when it blames, accuses, disapproves of, and 'punishes' others as well as itself.

What about loneliness? Is it also a negative emotion?

Loneliness—as opposed to aloneness—is a slow-burning negative emotion that also stems from our feeling of 'I'. The ego is what feels lonely, which is true because it isolates itself both physically and psychologically to protect itself. But Pure Being is not lonely. It transforms the heavy energy behind loneliness by seeing the ego clinging to it as a pillar of identity.

Loneliness can also unfurl into depression. Both have an instinctive foundation and a psychological layer on top of that foundation. The instinctive layer is associated with the nervous system, which is the infrastructure of the instinctive center. It may include sensations of tingling, tension, irritation, nausea, pain, or a general sense of unease or anxiety. All of this happens *in the body*.

The psychological layer happens *in the mind* as the sense of 'I' am lonely or 'I' am depressed. This is the emotional 'mood' that forms as a result of coarse, heavy energy seeping from the instinctive center into the emotional center where it infuses an atmosphere of gloom, apathy, hopelessness. The same energy can seep into the moving center where it causes lethargy, inertia, and immobility, as well as into the intellectual center where it prompts thoughts such as "what is this, why is it happening to me, what is wrong with me, what happens if this never goes away?" and so on.

It is possible to find your way out of the secondary layer of loneliness or depression by not taking it personally; by not buying into the urge to make it a problem that you need to be afraid of. From there you can try to see instinctive sensations as one thing, the emotional mood as another, the physical inertia as another, the sense of 'I' worrying about it and being afraid of it as another, and Pure Being as yet another. The space between all of these can 'open' and free the energy that is locked up in a negative emotion.

Something that may help is to visualize Pure Being stepping across the room and looking back at you and seeing your mind and body in the grip of the ego that is feeling lonely or depressed. What is being seen is not what is seeing it. This may not make depression dissolve right away, but it will prevent it from consuming you. Pure Being loses recognition by identifying with the sense of 'I' am feeling lonely and 'I' am feeling hopeless. Both are the ego. Try to notice this while also noticing that you are *being* aware of seeing it. Focus less on the feelings of 'I' am lonely and 'my' life is hopeless, and focus more on the realization that you can see the ego feeling those feelings without investing a sense of 'me' in them.

Negative emotions, whether they come in the form of depression or anger or resentment, all present the possibility for Pure Being to see the feeling of 'I' behind them as a mental projection that is obfuscating the recognition of the void of Pure Being. All negative emotions are bricks in the same wall. Pure Being is just beyond the wall. And the wall (which is the ego) is *imaginary*.

Isn't it also a matter of avoiding the conditions that make us negative?

The friction and pressure we encounter in our lives do not *cause* negative emotions. Negative emotions arise as a reaction to friction. Nothing external can *cause* negative emotions. They always stem from something that the ego adopts *in relation to itself* as an identity.

So other people don't make us negative?

Not directly. It is more that negative emotions attract negative emotions. They act like magnets for each other, but the reality of this goes unnoticed because everyone gets a strong dose of identity when there is an exchange of negativity. From the perspective of Pure Being, however, it is simply egos responding negatively to each other and to events *automatically*, with little or no awareness involved. However, when you don't respond to other people's identification and negativity with your own identification and negativity, this creates an added pressure because other people are expecting you to join them in the illusion. If you don't join them, they think you are odd or crazy or stubborn, which intensifies *their* identification. You then have to work your way through this pressure. But you cannot see the truth about the ego in other people before you see the same in yourself. It has to begin within you. Only then will you know how to navigate the social pressures of identification and negativity.

When you examine negative encounters with other people, you will see that it is the same tension and negativity that you encounter in yourself. There is a similar pressure in you and a similar fortitude you need to summon if you want to honor Pure Being. But the ego is afraid to deny other egos because it wants to be validated by them. This fear is part of the charade of life which is about egos seeking confirmation from other egos in a drama that has nothing to do with Pure Being. The most beautiful transformation of negative emotions and suffering is when no one else sees it happening. There is absolutely no room for the ego. Transformation is all about being for the sake of Pure Being.

The Place of Precious Things

I frequently experience negative emotions in the form of doubts that gnaw at me and become self-defeating. Sometimes they really scare me. What do you think is going on?

We all have demons of doubt about ourselves and about our spiritual growth. Such doubts are part of the smokescreen the ego throws up to protect itself. When the ego knows it is being exposed, it throws up instinctive and emotional 'ghosts' to fill the void of Pure Being. But it cannot succeed at this without cooperation from the void. The first few times you get pulled under, drawn into the storm, tossed around, think you are drowning, and feel afraid and doubtful. But after several roller coasters Pure Being will get its bearings. It will see the camouflage being set up and thrown in its direction, but it will recognize that as a trick of the ego and step out of the way. Then it will *completely* absorb those ghosts, those illusions.

This is possible because demons, doubts, and dark thoughts are just machinations of the mind projected as voices, images, emotions, sensations, and thoughts as part of the hologram of identity. It is the same hologram that all the great sages of history faced in themselves.

Many traditions speak about internal storms

and the 'dark night of the soul'. Sometimes they are called demons. Sometimes the devil. Sometimes temptations. But what do all these really mean? What are these thoughts, where do they come from, and why do they overwhelm us?

The fourth way offers an explanation that dismisses the idea of a devil or demons. It points instead to the instinctive center which operates behind the other three centers with an intelligence of its own. This is the center that governs our energy, supplies energy to the other centers, and monitors the body and mind to ensure their health and safety. Animals also have an instinctive center, but not an intellectual or emotional center, so they don't have a psychology. They don't experience the logic of thought or the fluctuation of emotion. They live simply to subsist and survive. Our instinctive center is the same, but it is tied to our psychology and ego, both of which it influences behind the scenes.

Dark thoughts, self-doubt, questioning the truth, and so on represent the ego resisting from its roots in the *negative half* of the instinctive center which produces a negative charge of energy. These psychological storms comprise a heady mix of sensations, thoughts, and emotions that together prove formidable as a defense mechanism of the ego which we feel as 'me' struggling with myself, doubting myself, and feeling hopeless. But it is all the ego. It is not Pure Being.

The purity of being sees internal storms but is not actually in them. Even if it finds itself wandering in the 'desert' of a storm it is not affected until it identifies with the storm and derives identity from the storm. As soon as it recognizes this, the storm cannot sway it, and this is the value of going through psychological trials. They can bolster the recognition of Pure Being.

When dogs growl and bark, are they experiencing negative emotions?

Their instinctive centers are negatively charged in those moments, but that does not translate into negative emotions because there is no psychological identity behind it. Human beings are also animals but with a more complex apparatus that includes an intellectual and an emotional center. Our instinctive center possesses the same venom you see in animals when they crouch, hiss, bark, growl, and show their teeth or raise their fur. We do the same, but in our case it gets mixed with emotional forms of irritation, anger, antagonism, blame, judgment, resentment, and so on that are tied to the ego.

Some animals also run away or burrow to protect themselves, which is what we do when we feel resentful or depressed. We are psychologically more complex than animals, but our reactions stem from the same *instinctive* foundation.

When you see behavior in yourself, and especially when you see negative emotions, try to distinguish what feels physical and what feels emotional. Try to see the link between the emotional feeling of 'me' and the instinctive center.

You mean how the instinctive center turns the emotional center in a negative direction?

Yes. How it infiltrates the emotional center. The emotional center is like water. Negative emotions are like ink that seep into the water. The ink comes from the instinctive center and permeates the emotional center as well as the intellectual center. Self-pity turns the water gray, irritation makes it violet, anger makes it red, depression turns it black. Without the ink of negative emotions, the water would be pure all the time. Nothing fancy. Just clear.

When the 'ink' of the instinctive centers seeps into the emotional center, you can dissolve it by adding chemicals in the form of attitudes, or spend hours and days at a time sifting the water with a net of psychological cures and practices. Or you can wave the magic wand of Pure Being over the water and watch the ink disappear.

When the emotional center operates in clear 'water', what we experience are not positive emotions, but what might be called pleasant emotions because as soon as they get tainted by unpleasant energy from the instinctive center they can turn negative. In other words, they are still vulnerable to infiltration.

The term 'positive emotion' in the fourth way refers to something else. It means Pure Being recognizing itself above, below, and around the four centers and the sense of 'I' they generate. Positive emotions emanate from this recognition and have a positive charge that cannot be reversed by the instinctive center because positive emotions have no sense of identity attached to them.

You make it sound easy, but negative emotions are not so easy to control.

They are not easy to control because they are the most volatile energy produced by the body and mind, and because the ego is fueled by that volatility. The ego reaches its strongest levels of intensity and rigidity through negative emotions. And the specific kind of negative emotion, and whether it is active or passive, is not important. What matters is the energy behind it because this energy is what can be transmuted as pure conscious *being*. For Pure Being, negative emotions contain the energy—the substance—of itself before that energy formed into the ego through the process of identification.

Some people say that transformation involves eating negative emotions. Is that accurate?

Pure Being does not 'eat' negative emotions as such. It cracks the shell of the ego and tosses the shell aside, which defuses the negative emotion. Then it consumes the energy of what *had become* negative emotions.

Is resistance an aspect of negativity?

Resistance is a recoil of the four centers in response to pressure. It becomes psychologically negative only when 'I' gets attached to it.

For example, the instinctive center feels pain, awareness identifies with it as 'I' feel pain, followed by a feeling in the emotional center of 'I' am afraid of pain or 'I' am angry that it hurts or why is this happening to 'me'.

Transformation comes when Pure Being detaches and withdraws from the sense of 'I'. This enables the energy behind the negative emotion to funnel back to Pure Being where it gets absorbed *as* Pure Being. When Pure Being transforms a negative emotion such as irritation, what funnels back is not the irritation but the energy which had gathered around the sense of 'I' as irritation. When the nucleus of 'I' is seen as an illusion, the nucleus dissolves, the form of the emotion clinging to it disintegrates, the negative energy behind it gets released, and as it starts to rise and return to Pure Being its 'charge' transforms from negative to positive, bringing with it a relief and lightness of being.

Why don't you endorse psychotherapy as a tool for transformation?

Psychotherapy usually tries to address each negative emotion by teaching you how to adjust your sense of 'me' so as not to give rise to that emotion. But this only reinforces the sense of 'me', 'my' problem, and 'my' attempts to fix it in 'myself'. The fourth way takes the approach that negative emotions are different in terms of their content and manifestation, but *exactly* the same in terms of what is behind them and how they act as camouflage for the 'I' and 'me' of ego. What traditional therapy misses is the recognition that there is something behind the ego which is the void of Pure Being, that *this* is the source of resolution, and that transformation can never happen in or to the mind. The mind is just an arena in which negative emotions entertain and sustain the ego.

But therapy can at least tame strong emotions.

Sometimes that is true, but even then it is happening in the mind as an adjustment of the ego which remains relatively intact. Meanwhile, negative emotions usually unfold so fast that you don't see them coming or see where they came from until they are on top of you. This is certainly the case with explosive anger. On the other hand, a negative emotion like depression can unfold so slowly that you don't recognize it until it is undermining your energy and mood.

Like all negative emotions, anger and depression are hard to detect as they form because they form out of material from the instinctive center which is elusive to perception.

Always remember that Pure Being in you is not depressed. It is simply that Pure Being is identified with your idea of yourself, your problems, your suffering, and your impulse to retreat into an oppressive condition to protect your idea of yourself, which is *only an idea*. This is another serious limitation of therapy: it considers the ego to be a real identity, to be you.

When Pure Being is unconscious it clings to the rope of depression (or any other negative emotion) because it thinks it is holding onto itself in the form of identity. It does not know that all it has to do is let go of the rope of 'I' and float to the surface. The truth is that it does not even have to float to the surface because when it consciously realizes itself it is immediately at the surface of (in the void of) itself.

Can you say more about the two layers of depression?

It is easy to get depressed about being depressed, which compounds the depression. The same is true about anger. It easy to get angry about being angry. If you see this and back out of the secondary layer, you will be better able to withdraw from the primary layer. It sounds contradictory, but don't get depressed about the fact that you are feeling depressed. Or angry about having been angry. Instead, look squarely at the depression and anger. Notice not only the physical and psychological effects they have on you, but notice the feeling of 'I' that is feeling these effects and taking them personally.

Depression is anchored in the instinctive center. From there it infiltrates the other centers and depletes their energy. When you examine this with a clear lens you find Pure Being holding onto a long rope that is tied to the ocean bottom of the instinctive center. Awareness is clinging to that rope because it is identified, and the deeper it follows the rope, the stronger the sense of 'I' becomes. It gets murky down there, so Pure Being has a hard time distinguishing itself from the heavy emotions, their instinctive roots, and the convincing sense of ego they perpetuate.

That uncertainty also seems to produce a lot of anxiety.

Low-level anxiety and the tension it creates are like pilot lights of identification. They make it easy for identification to burst into flame. Turn off the pilot light on your stove and see what happens when you try to light it. Nothing. Remember, too, that Pure Being is *never* anxious.

Is anxiety a malfunction of the instinctive center that is due to identification?

Yes. The current of identification is an unconscious form of energy from Pure Being that rifles through the four centers which respond by getting agitated and exaggerated. For instance, you start rushing, talking fast, speaking with vehemence, worrying, imagining the worst, overeating, overthinking. You get completely absorbed in a principle or cause or problem or person and shut yourself inside the walls of that topic of identification. All of these effects happen as the *contents* of the four centers. But you can also feel identification as a vibration in the *structure* of each center. And instead of trying to control their contents—their reactions—you can focus on the structure of the centers and disconnect the plug there by aligning their structures with the resonance of Pure Being.

Is that the only way out?

You can also get out of anxiety and other negative emotions by realizing that you are seeing them circulate inside. You calm down by not identifying with and not interfering with them. Don't try *not* to be anxious. Just try not to identify with the anxiety you see and feel. The instinctive center and chief feature want you to jump in with identification. Don't bend your hooks around that urge. Just keep looking with the clear vision of pure light. As bright a light as you can be.

It also helps to remember how negative emotions build and perpetuate themselves in layers. We become negative, then we identity with being negative, then we become negative with ourselves for being negative. Try to stop at the first layer. Just feel the negative instinctive energy in the body and look at the psychological entity that is getting upset. This chain of chemical reactions taking place inside can only compound itself in the dark. As soon as you cast the light of Pure Being on it, the chemical balance starts to change. When you shine full light on it, the material forming as your sense of identity will dissolve. The void of Pure Being will just *be* here.

Once I see a negative emotion why can't I shake it off and get rid of it?

Sometimes when we know we are irritable or in a bad mood, we say 'I' cannot shake it off. This is because the ego is trying to shake off the *reaction* in the four centers. It wants to feel better but does not understand that it is the problem causing the problem and that the source of both problems is identification.

When the voltage of identification is intense, it can also take time for the centers to neutralize and normalize. But you can feel it starting right away. You can feel the energy changing. It is like lowering the temperature on the stove.

Are negative emotions part of the ego or separate from the ego?

They exist by themselves but they operate in conjunction with the ego. They serve as an extension of the ego, a promulgation of the ego, and a defense mechanism of the ego which projects itself internally and externally through the expression of negative emotions. All these projections give the impression that the ego is more substantial and more powerful than it really is.

The ego is just a manifestation of energy in the psyche that has no solid basis other than identification. When you take away identification, the energy behind the ego dissipates and loses its capacity to project images of itself, especially images of itself as negative emotions.

Is this true of all emotions; that they work in conjunction with the ego?

Negative emotions originate in the instinctive center as a negative charge of energy that gets transported to the emotional center via identification. In most cases this energy accumulates in the negative half of the instinctive center as a reaction to pressure and unsatisfied desires. When it turns into a negative emotion it does so as an irritated and unhappy ego.

Simple pure emotions, on the other hand, do not form as reactions. They arise in response to the awareness of Pure Being. But most people experience more negative emotions than pure emotions because they spend the majority of their lives identified as their ego rather than in their natural essence. Essence also has a sense of identity, but it is very naive and pure compared to the ego of personality, and even when it becomes negatively charged it is not vehemently defensive or destructive. The negative charge does take a psychological hold over it.

Negative emotions do not form at all in the dimension of Pure Being for the simple reason that there is no identification and no identity for them to form around.

So negative emotions cannot develop without an ego?

That's right. Negative emotions start as a sensation that turns into a feeling which combusts and takes shape as 'I'. The ego forms first and creates a channel for negativity to flow through.

Negative emotions then circulate through that channel and energize the ego. They are hard to stop because they are so fast. They form and immediately combust. But we can slow things down by not expressing them through the four centers and by understanding why this is significant. It is like giving ourselves time to get to a bomb and defuse the detonator before it explodes. Once it explodes it is too late.

Thoughts also arise out of energy and take shape as the ego, right?

Yes, but they are a slower, denser form of energy. It is one thing to transcend a thought. It is another to transcend a volatile emotion. The process is the same but the speed and combustibility are very different. Pure Being has to be ahead of a negative emotion. It has to recognize itself before recognizing the emotion. This is why negative emotions pose such a challenge. Pure Being has to be in the foreground as well as the background and has to remain in both if it is to transcend and transform negative emotions.

In this sense, the purpose of not expressing negative emotions is not to get rid of them. The purpose is to contain their energy so it can be transformed. Pure Being transforms this energy by siphoning it back into itself. As that happens negative emotions rid themselves of themselves.

If you feel like you are struggling with negative emotions and struggling with yourself having them, it is because you are still identified with the feeling of 'I' behind the negative emotion. Try to distinguish between the energy of the negative emotion, the feeling of 'I' am negative, and the feeling of 'I' am struggling with 'my' negativity. This last one is also a negative emotion, especially when it takes the form of 'I' am a failure because I cannot control and transform my negative emotions—which is a perfect attitude concocted by the ego to sustain itself as the sense of self.

When we do contain the energy behind negative emotions, what happens next?

Withholding the expression of a negative emotion contains the energy behind it, and this in turn creates an internal pressure that exposes the feeling of 'I' which is the ego. As Pure Being transcends the feeling of 'I' by not identifying with it, the sense of identity in the negative emotion falls apart and releases the energy behind it.

This energy which had originally belonged to Pure Being before it became identified with sensations and emotions returns to its source in the void, and this transforms *the void.*

And that's true with all negative emotions?

The form negative emotions take and the way they get expressed—even by different people in different nations—is basically the same because the instinctive center and how the ego forms in conjunction with it is the same. *All* negative emotions are part of the same invisible belt that keeps humanity bound together in the unconsciousness of being.

I just had an image of everyone around the world jumping into negative emotions instead of jumping out of them.

It's very close to the truth. When a negative emotion arises, we usually react by going deeper into the emotion without any intent to resolve it. We are already identified and then we identify with the negative emotion. Deeper and deeper we go. Instead, we could turn the other direction and rise into Pure Being—as Pure Being—with the intent of transcending both the negative emotion and the feeling of 'I' experiencing the negative emotion. But that requires not identifying with the feeling of ego inside the negative emotion. Non-identification neutralizes the polarity of Pure Being by turning away from negative emotions and letting mind activity and bodily concerns take care of themselves without indulging in them. There is no attempt at solutions or resolutions. There is just Pure Being recognizing what is happening.

From the way you describe it, it sounds like we need negative emotions even though they are just projections of the ego.

You need negative emotions until you no longer need them. There will no longer be any juice to squeeze out of them. You will know.

The fourth way goes into considerable detail about transformation, particularly the transformation of negative emotions. Why do you think other teachings don't do the same thing?

The idea of self-transformation is ancient, but it may be that detailed knowledge about how negative emotions form in the human psyche and how non-expression can be used as a lever for transformation became necessary due to the rise of industrial societies in the late nineteenth and early twentieth centuries. A case can be made that burgeoning populations, large numbers of people living and working in cities, and the intense pressure put on instinctive centers to compete in the industrial and now technical world has resulted in a more complicated ego which *has to* rely more on negative emotions to sustain itself.

If this is true, a system of knowledge like the fourth way that explains the ego in detail became necessary. It had to be a system that could be brought to bear in daily life rather than in the isolation of a monastery or ashram or cave. It also had to incorporate long-standing truths while appealing to a western-educated mind that was unfamiliar with the language and philosophy of eastern traditions and no longer connected to the esoteric meaning behind the great religions. Above all, it had to be a system of knowledge that is practical *for the mind* because the intellectual center is better equipped to influence the emotional center than the instinctive and moving centers are.

Do you see any correlation between what you just described and the state of mental health today?

Yes. It is no accident that we have been seeing a steady rise in the commercialism of psychology and psychotherapy. Yet they do not have all the answers to the concern and confusion that more and more people are having about identity. This also seems to be why there is a significant upsurge of interest in spirituality. Not because people are hungering for reality, but because they want to resolve conflicts in their psyche. We see this, too, when meditation and yoga are used primarily to lower stress, tension, and anxiety, as opposed to being vehicles for the self-realization—the recognition—of Pure Being.

Where does transformation lead?

What looks like transformation to the mind is essentially breathing for Pure Being. It inhales everything. Transformation means drawing everything into the void of Pure Being and resolving it as Pure Being. What remains after negative emotions and suffering have been transformed is the untainted consciousness of Pure Being. It is then free to transform everything in creation.

Can you suggest a reliable method for thinking about and dealing with emotions in general?

Think of emotions, especially negative emotions, as rooms in your psychological house. Envision yourself as Pure Being visiting each room and taking on the feeling of 'I' that each room exudes. For instance, there is the living room of judgment where we spend a lot of time, the basement of resentment, the dungeon of depression, the outhouse of guilt, and the rooms of different shades of color such as anxiety, suspicion, fear, anger, jealousy, self-pity, worry. Which rooms do you habitually find yourself in? Is there a common theme or feeling of 'I' they contribute to? What would happen if you walked down the hall, out the front door, and completely out of town?

Negative emotions occupy a lot of our time because they are given such a great deal of credence, even by professionals.

It is peculiar how humanity views negative emotions and the business of expressing them as normal, healthy, necessary, and even beneficial. Only when you break negative emotions down do you see how abnormal and corrupt they are, especially in terms of how they obscure, distort, and displace Pure Being. Only then do you see what it means to be 'asleep' and that negative emotions *keep us* asleep.

You said negative emotions deny reality. Can you explain that a little more?

The energy of what *will become* negative emotions starts as a reaction in the instinctive center, but it takes shape as a response in the emotional center. In this sense, each negative emotion is a psychological convulsion followed by a physical regurgitation—the expression—of an *undigested* perception. To put it another way, each negative emotion rejects reality and its rejection is as powerful as the corresponding reality is true. The more explosive a negative emotion is, the more potent is the truth behind it that is being rejected and deflected. But this gets overlooked because the negative half of the emotional center enjoys the intensity and volatility of negative emotions. In partnership with the ego, it likes to vent negativity as a way of beating others down and proving itself right.

But in a strange way it feels so good.

Expressing negative emotions feels good because it releases volatile energy. The instinctive and the emotional centers feel relieved of a burden. It also feels good because the volatility of negativity has been used by the ego as a demonstration of its strength and as a weapon for threatening and hurting and controlling and punishing the psyche of other egos, or as way of persuading itself that its personal needs warrant special attention or pity. What gets missed in all these instances is how negative energy swells into a psychological wave that the ego rides as negative emotions. The ego paddles out again and again and rides wave after wave back to the shore of identity.

It also feels right to assign blame where blame is due, despite the fact that it can be negative.

As much as it seems right to assign blame and then apply it through the expression of negative emotions, ultimately no one is to blame because everything we do happens as unconscious manifestations of the instinctive center and the ego, which together generate the notion of being the person of 'me'. Transformation resides above this notion in the dimension of Pure Being. Identification with hurt and resentment, no matter how painful, keeps you in a lower dimension where the hurt and resentment can never be resolved on their terms. That is what blame and retribution are: futile attempts to resolve differences on the level on which they occurred. But even when it works it appeases only the ego.

What does true resolution look like?

As Pure Being identifies again and again and again with sensations, thoughts, feelings, and negative emotions it accumulates around them and takes on their vibration. By identifying with them, it imbues itself and them with the feeling of 'I'. When Pure Being recognizes *itself*, it withdraws identification with the mind and body. It draws back into itself, and the feeling of 'I' dissipates. Rather than the ego trying to resolve things, it *gets resolved* as Pure Being.

Why do we feel such a compulsion to be on the go all the time?

Most people are not accustomed to being silent and still because the body and mind feel a constant urge to be doing and thinking, which promotes a feeling of identity. In general, the stronger a person's personality is, the more urgently they need to move and think.

Why do you think relationships have a way of getting generally worse rather than better?

Human relations get muddy because they are ego-based and ego-driven. The ego wants things from another person that will make it feel secure. The other person becomes an object of need, desire, and affirmation. From there dependency grows in mutually reinforcing ways. When the ego does not get what it wants, it rebels and a friend becomes an enemy, and the ego feeds off that. Amazingly, this is what the ego is designed to do. It is why it was built into the human psyche—to *promote* identification.

It remains rare to find an unidentified human who is free of ego and does not expect, require, or demand anything from anyone. It is not even that they are free of ego. It is that the illusion of ego has dissolved the way a cloud dissolves to reveal the sun that had only appeared to be obscured. Its light then shines with unconditional openness and fullness.

We often seem to choose problems over freedom.

Ironically, everyone is trying to be free. Most

people are just choosing the wrong kind of freedom and the wrong door to freedom because their choosing is being driven by the ego which in turn is being driven by the instinctive center—all in the name of 'I' want to be free, happy, fulfilled.

True freedom and happiness, however, do not mean constant comfort, buoyancy, or excitement. They mean the absence of attachment and the absence of unhappiness, and the absence of any reason to be attached or unhappy—which means the absence of ego.

What is a good way to confront and overcome feelings of discouragement?

Try to see those feelings as objects; as artificial limbs on the mannequin of ego which you mistake yourself to be. Although it is human nature to feel discouraged, this is just another way the ego stays in charge as the feeling of 'I'. Pure Being, on the other hand, never feels that way. It is free of discouragement, just as it is free of hope. The trouble is that it is usually identified with thoughts and feelings and their common thread of 'I'. So it is not a matter of dissuading or overcoming discouragement. It is a matter of transcending the notion of 'I' who feels discouraged. This kind of freedom can never be imposed on the world because it has to emerge in each human as a result of the non-identification and conscious self-realization of Pure Being.

I feel like I should be able to conquer my impulse to feel discouraged about my disappointments.

None of the 'I's or 'my's in your statement is Pure Being. Those are the ego, which likes a good fight, especially a noble one. And being the winner or loser does not matter because either way the notion of self gets attention, affirmation, and reinforcement. The ego achieves the same thing by imposing expectations and demands on other people and then depending on others to reinforce its sense of 'I'. This can take different forms such as control, fear, deference, intimidation, worship, and so on. The form does not matter. What matters is that the ego appears to be a real person and that it establishes itself in relationship to other egos and uses those relationships to fortify its image of itself as an individual. It is strange to realize that this is happening to everyone regardless of their brand of ego and negative emotions.

What's the best way to respond when I get falsely accused?

When the world hurls an accusation at the ego, it stings, it hurts, it sticks, and it leaves a mark. If there is no ego, whatever gets hurled just keeps going—nowhere.

Aren't some forms of depression legitimate?

Depression can take different forms, but all of them are negative emotions that usually stem from two things: the instinctive center feeling pressured or unsatisfied or unsatiated, and the emotional center feeling discontent or deprived or distraught. Together, the negative halves of the instinctive and emotional centers form a wall of psychological resistance which the ego embodies as *the idea* of 'me' under pressure, unsatisfied, distraught. The ego uses this stronghold as a barricade, a shield, and a justification. The 'person' may or may not realize the root of what is bothering them, and even when they do they are often reluctant to avoid it or find a remedy because the ego does not have a better alternative to sustain itself, and because it is afraid to fall into the void of no identity. The phantom 'me' does not want to dissolve into the reality of Pure Being. This is true of all negative emotions and the feeling of 'me' behind them.

At the same time, there are some intense human emotions that are not negative as such until they get appropriated by the ego. For example, grief and loss. These are emotions that penetrate essence and are felt as deep emotional pain. They are strong reminders of the fragility and vulnerability of the human form, and in this they have an important purpose because they inform us about our humanity and the impermanence of the mind and body. A similar kind of emotion happens when a person receives a severe diagnosis. All these kinds of emotions come as big shocks that rattle us at our core. They knock the ego off its pedestal. They punch essence in the face. And most importantly, they can awaken the recognition of Pure Being.

What happens in many if not most cases, however, is that these emotions get appropriated by the ego which resists and denies the reality of the circumstances that led to them. The ego takes the emotions personally and in doing so corrupts the explosive charge they carry. It turns what is potentially a fuel for profound perception into runaway negative emotions that reject and deny and remain bitter about reality.

Intense emotions of this kind are also rare in most people's lives and, although they are difficult to bear, they do not last. They strike and soon start to dissipate. For instance, strong grief turns into a period of mourning, which turns into periodic sad moments, which turn into occasional bitter-sweet memories. This is the course they run in essence.

But things are different in the ego of personality which wants to hold onto the pain, the self-pity, the anger, the fear, and so on. The ego keeps chewing on what was originally the rarefied substance of a big 'shock' and makes it denser and denser, more and more negative. And it feels right to 'me' to do this. It feels legitimate. Meanwhile it keeps Pure Being bound to the mind and body in the form of an ego.

Are appreciation and gratitude examples of positive emotions?

Emotions of appreciation and gratitude can be authentic, yet they remain vulnerable to infection from the instinctive center. One day you love life and other people. The next day you hate them and blame them. True positive emotions, however, are not subject to just one side of the picture, so they do not flip to their opposite. They arise from seeing things as they are. The word 'posit' means to position. Positive emotions arise from seeing the true position of things within the whole—the void—of reality.

Why do you think people get so negative about god and religion, especially about other people's gods and religions?

It is hard for people to accept that god is a mind-made idea embroidered by mind-made forms of religion which become safeguards of belief, ritual, guilt, punishment, penance, forgiveness, and dependence. To stay upright, the ego has to defend its particular structures of belief. Many egos would get very upset if you took these structures away, yet reality exists without all of them.

It is strange that religion unknowingly reinforces negative emotions.

Yes, and not just religion. Nearly all of life endorses the validity and the need for negative emotions. Consider how many people around the globe are suffering right now from guilt and anger and depression and think it rational to do so, which keeps them mired in it. Meanwhile, Pure Being looms just beyond that mire unaware of being there—*right here.* All it has to do is recognize itself, yet this remains rare in humanity.

The Psychology of the Ego

The Place of Precious Things

If the doors of perception were cleansed,
everything would appear to man as it is,
Infinite.

William Blake

You sometimes mention the idea of body types and how that affects people's behavior. Can you talk a little about this?

According to the fourth way, each person's physiological and psychological traits stem from being one of seven 'body types' which are influenced by the five interior planets, the sun, and the moon. Each type is named after the planetary body from which it derives its attributes of size, speed, constitution, and metabolism. For example, mercurial types are small, fast, and luminous like the planet Mercury. Martial types are often red-haired, rugged, and plain. Jovials (Jupiter) are large, rotund, colorful, and profound. Saturns are distant, guarded, and circumspect. Lunars are secretive, cold, and consistent. Each of the types is characterized by a mixture of physical makeup, psychological tendencies, and social demeanor.

Is this tied to the concept of personality types?

There are several popular concepts of 'personality types' which are loosely based on the enneagram. They are offshoots of the fourth way theory, but other than that they share nothing in common with the original delineation of body types, or what the types represent, or what their celestial influence signifies. Personality types are also laid out on all nine points of the enneagram, whereas the scheme of body types is laid out across just six points on the circle of the enneagram, plus a point in the middle that refers to the sun. The three other points on the enneagram which form a triangle are not related to body types; they belong to a separate symbol within the enneagram.

What do you mean that it is an offshoot?

I mean it is based on the original idea but in an incomplete and distorted way. For instance, the idea of personality types does not point to its source, to what determines personality, whereas the fourth way links body types to glands and glands to planetary influences. The idea of 'personality types' also presumes nine or more types, but that is a misinterpretation of how the enneagram was designed as *two diagrams in one symbol*. The fourth way includes only seven types. The concept of 'personality types' also frames things strictly in terms of behavior while the fourth way explains that 'body type' refers to a person's essence when they are born, which includes the tendencies of chief feature. A personality develops around essence based on the race, culture, language, family, education, and religion a person grows up in. The inherent tendency of chief feature is always there in essence, but its manifestations in personality take on different hues according to the environment it develops in.

Many people nowadays use the idea of 'personality types' to characterize the personal traits of themselves and others. But the information about body types is not intended to explain who you are. It is intended to cast as bright a light as possible on what Pure Being *is not*. The purpose of the body type model is not to substantiate the character of 'I', but to expose the psychological infrastructure on which 'I' is built.

The fourth way also explains other things that influence our appearance, preferences, and behavior. One of these is how, in addition to body type, each person has a 'center of gravity' in one of the four centers. There may be four people of the same body type, but one is centered in the instinctive center, one in the moving center, one in the intellectual center, and one in the emotional center. Even though they share the same body type, each of them anticipates, acts, and reacts differently according to their center of gravity which adds a specific shade and nuance to their body type.

What do you mean by 'chief feature'?

Each type in the fourth way system has an underlying chemical impulse that drives a person's mental outlook, proclivities, and preferences. This impulse governs their viewpoint, decisions, values, and human interactions to such an extent that the fourth way calls it chief weakness or chief 'feature' because it is at the same time a strength, a limitation, and a blind spot. For instance, saturnine types who are governed by a tendency toward deep thought and social dominance see themselves and the world differently than lunar types who are governed by resilience and stubbornness. Meanwhile, jovial types, who are governed by conviviality and vanity, see things differently than both saturns and lunars, as do mercurials and martials and venusians and solars, each of whom have their own distinct features. Needless to say, differences in body type, center of gravity, and chief feature play a significant role in the inability of human beings to understand, empathize with, and cooperate with others in every walk of life across every culture and continent.

Some of the personality type systems also talk about the strengths and weaknesses of each type. Is that the same thing as chief feature?

What the fourth way calls 'chief feature' is more than simply strengths and weaknesses and traits. It is an inborn predisposition in the mind which regulates our psychological outlook, preferences, and decisions. Chief feature has roots in the instinctive center, but it sprouts from there as an overriding tendency in the mind. Together, the instinctive center and chief feature create a platform for the ego to stand on and make its case as a substitute for pure conscious being.

The chief feature of vanity, for example, is the feeling of being unique. It can unfold as pride or self-doubt. These are the two sides of vanity. For instance, you may feel uniquely handsome or uniquely ugly, uniquely gifted or uniquely awkward, and so on. Either way vanity establishes a position and then judges itself and others from that position. At the same time, everyone has vanity in the sense that everyone's chief feature is vain about itself. Ironically, vanity helps mask the fact that chief feature is chief feature. For instance, we as the ego get irritated by other people's vanity, but it is not their vanity that causes the irritation. It is ours. Our vanity is irritated and our irritation camouflages this truth.

You said chief feature regulates our outlook and decisions. Can you give an example?

Chief feature is a deep impulse that drives the psychological engine of our reactions which in turn become the primary cloak of the ego. For instance, some of us naturally tend toward control, some toward avoidance, some toward fear, some toward laziness. We cannot help but act and react from this core tendency because it flows through our blood and has a chemical influence on our psychology. In doing so it serves as an axle for our sense of 'I' to develop around. This is why we used to say, "You don't have a chief feature; you *are* chief feature." Chief feature is hard to see in ourselves because we *are it*. Benjamin Franklin noticed this when he recorded that he felt proud about curtailing his most prominent foible which was pride.

Another common feature is 'power' which manifests as a person who is always charging in, being bossy, taking over. Their impulse is to wield power. But suppose this person grows up in a family or culture where this is frowned upon. Instead of the feature resorting to its normal inclinations, it manifests instead through frustration and destructiveness. Instead of the feature directly controlling others, it criticizes them, accuses them, and tries to destroy them socially or professionally.

Another classic feature is 'vanity' which manifests as an urge toward self-aggrandizement that leads to attention-getting. Sometimes this is tolerated by others, sometimes not. When it is not, it switches from being offensive to being defensive, such as by needing to prove itself, always insisting on being right, and taking everything—especially criticism—personally and accusatorily.

Pride and shame are both forms of self-indulgence that lead to self-preoccupation. One is the positive side of vanity. The other is the negative side. People who have a chief feature of vanity often slip between the two, feeling great about themselves one day and terrible the next. Vanity also loves to play the victim and be the victim, which it can also do in conjunction with any other feature. Most people are proud of their chief feature without knowing that the feature of vanity is compounding their chief feature.

So how does this become a platform for the ego?

Our feeling of identity gets established in the mind as an image that remains primarily inward facing, caught up in itself, projecting itself from within itself out into the world. Both internally and externally, this projection is laced with the energy of chief feature which then manifests as the impulse to do something, to make things happen or prevent them from happening, or to control or resist them when they do happen. Without realizing it, chief feature always manages to get in the way, either actively or passively. But it does not purposely oppose Pure Being because it is not conscious of itself or of Pure Being. It simply runs contrary to Pure Being. It tries to pull and push reality whereas Pure Being watches reality manifest in its natural course.

Is there a way to get rid of it and just be ourselves?

You cannot get rid of chief feature. It is part of your fabric as a human being. What you *can* minimize is the habit of identifying with the feeling of 'I' it perpetuates and the behavior it promotes, which includes the urge to get rid of chief feature and to become negative when you cannot. All of that is the ego revolving around chief feature.

People also ask how they can control chief feature, which would appear to be the goal but is not. Part of the reason why not is because it is like asking how to overpower power, or how not to be afraid of fear, or how to shy away from shyness. In other words, it is a question being asked from the feature itself, from inside the feature—which is very common for the simple reason that chief feature influences even how we think about chief feature.

The real goal is to see the full extent to which chief feature influences our thoughts, decisions, actions, and preferred negative emotions. This is important because we cannot pinpoint 'I' itself. 'I' is a psychological hologram. But it can be detected in the way it manifests through chief feature, particularly how chief feature recoils into negative emotions to defend itself.

I have a feeling that my chief feature is not a very pleasant one.

There are no pleasant features, and it does not

matter what your chief feature is, just like it does not matter what kind of negative emotions you are prone to. What matters is seeing the mental projection—the image—of 'I' behind them.

Gurdjieff suggested trying not to express the 'involuntary manifestations' of chief feature, which is noteworthy because this is the same principle behind not expressing negative emotions. You cannot necessarily stop a negative emotion from forming in the mind, but you can control its outward expression. The same is true about chief feature. You cannot control its underlying impulse, but you can *minimize* its external manifestations, and doing so can promote the transformation of Pure Being.

With both negative emotions and chief feature, not expressing them means putting brakes on the momentum of 'I' in the psychological world before it takes flight in the physical world. This is spiritual self-denial. It means denying your false self the chance to breathe on its own as the notion of a person. A small example is keeping your mouth shut when you feel inclined to criticize or correct or override someone else.

But just staying quiet can create moments of awkward silence.

As personalities we have developed a feeling of insecurity when there is silence. The ego has learned to fill the void with a projection of itself either in the mind or through talking, fidgeting, joking, whistling, or looking down. When there is silence, most people do not know what to fall back on other than the impulses of chief feature. And this happens only between human beings. We never experience it with pets, for example. *Only in relation to humans do we feel the need to protect our sense of identity.*

When you find yourself in moments of awkward silence, let them linger without interrupting the silence. It will give you a clear view of imaginary 'I'. Let the feeling of awkwardness rise without deflecting it. Try to silently 'ride' the pressure it creates. This is the same approach as not expressing negative emotions. By not expressing them you tap into the energy behind them and resolve that energy as Pure Being.

What is the connection between chief feature and negative emotions?

All features shield themselves behind a particular group of negative emotions. Power tends toward one type of negativity, vanity another, and fear another. Between Pure Being and the surge of a negative emotion there is a gap that is usually filled by chief feature rushing in to declare or camouflage or defend itself. When you withhold the expression of negativity, or allow moments of awkward silence, this gap widens. If you understand this and let the gap open wide enough, it becomes a door through which Pure Being can realize itself more fully. Said another way, the more this gap widens, the more it can fill with Pure Being, and the more it fills with Pure Being the more consciously Pure Being recognizes and realizes itself.

You also said that center of gravity adds color to a person's body type. Do you mean that it is an aspect of their type?

Not an aspect. Just an added filter. All four centers get woven around chief feature, but one of them forms as a thicker strand than the others. The fourth way calls this 'center of gravity' because in each person one of the four centers exerts more 'pull' over a person's interests, actions, and reactions. Their outlook and the course of their life is then governed by either sensation, movement, emotion, or thought.

As with body type, center of gravity is also part of essence, so it influences your physical makeup as well as your mental outlook. For instance, people centered in the intellectual center typically have a wiry frame whereas emotionally centered people tend to be noticeably fleshy. Moving types are often lean and athletic compared to instinctive types who are more 'thick' and sensual.

When Pure Being extracts its awareness from identification, the apparatus of chief feature, center of gravity, and all four centers starts to operate differently. It is the same apparatus with the same traits and tendencies but without the injection of 'me'. But as long as Pure Being is identified, chief feature is pumping the apparatus of ego full of 'me', 'me', 'me'. As this material of 'me' flows out of the ego, it does so through all four centers, but primarily through our center of gravity which steers our interests and behavior.

How can we determine someone's chief feature?

Sometimes a feature is as apparent as the classic name for it, such as willfulness, which means a stubborn insistence to always do things your way on your terms. Chief feature may also be less apparent, so it is better described in terms of the nuance with which it manifests. For instance, willfulness may take the form of "always finding a reason to resist or say no."

The feature of dominance, as the name implies, stems from the impulse to be overbearing, controlling, and condescending. But in some cases it might be more aptly called, "likes to have the final word about everything," or simply, "Miss know-it-all."

Each feature remains locked in the prison of its own making convinced that the impulse and outlook it perpetuates are legitimate.

Is chief feature what makes us feel so separate from other people?

Partly, yes. The instinctive center and chief feature both exist *in relation to* people and this fosters a strong sense of being separate. Feeling separate physically and psychologically provides security, but it is not relationships that do this; it is the contrast which relationships provide. Experiencing yourself *in relation to* people establishes and reinforces the feeling of self.

Chief feature also measures people against itself and uses its standards as a basis for judging others. At the same time it escapes from being judged by allowing itself to think it is right no matter what position it finds itself in. Whatever you do or think, you get to be right. People wonder why the world is the way it is. This is a large part of the reason. Everyone is right and thinks everyone else is wrong, which has not changed in humanity for tens of thousands of years.

I thought the ego is responsible for making us feel separate?

In a way you are right because the instinctive center and chief feature do not have identity by themselves. One is just an organism. The other is just a tendency. It is only when they get infused with identification that they develop a sense of self as the ego. They become the central fixture around which the ego forms, animates, and projects itself. The ego, governed by chief feature, also learns about the concept of chief feature. It then derives pleasure from seeing features in other people and ridiculing them for it, even though it does not know why it likes this, and without knowing that it is seeing other people through the lens of its own chief feature.

What do you mean by different shades and nuances of chief feature and center of gravity?

Imagine energy as water flowing through our mind and body. At certain points along the way, chief feature and center of gravity release different chemicals and colors into the water. The water looks different, tastes different, and acts differently in different people, but it is the same water. It just takes on different flavors.

We are not as unique as the ego thinks we are. We all have the same energy of Pure Being passing through us, but it is colored by our body type, chief feature, and center of gravity.

Why isn't all this more apparent?

Between the different compartments of the ego there are psychological cushions. The fourth way calls them 'buffers' because they stand between our contradictions and soften the transition we experience when passing between contradictory sides of our nature. Each buffer is on a swivel made up of lightning-quick reflexes in the instinctive and emotional centers. These reflexes enable us to turn away from one side of ourselves and into another without realizing what is happening. Even chief feature cannot discern its own buffers.

Can you give an example of a buffer?

Buffers are like blinders. They keep you looking straight ahead without seeing anything else. For instance, 'I's that want to diet swivel into 'I's that think, "Well, it's alright to have this ice cream." These different 'I's don't come into conflict because they are not seen together. The buffer-reflex dodges the contradiction. Some 'I's want to smoke while other 'I's want to give up smoking and are sure they can, but they have never talked to the 'I's that want to keep smoking, just as 'I's that do cruel things to other people have never spoken to the 'I's that say, "That is not me. I would never do that." But then the first group of 'I's does it again and the cycle repeats itself without any recognition of Pure Being behind it. Each 'I' that springs from the ego thinks it is the singular 'I' only to vanish as soon as the ego swivels and switches into another 'I'.

A buffer can take the form of a thought, such as "It is okay to have some potato chips." But at their root, buffers are a reflex; either an instinctive or a psychological reflex, or a combination of both. The buffer usually happens so fast that you don't see the reflex. You see only what it allows, which is another way to describe buffers. They *allow us* to go against ourselves, to contradict ourselves, to hide from ourselves, to shield ourselves from the reality of things and from the truth about the ego.

Buffers play a large role in our life behind the scenes. They deflect the truth about the contradictory sides of the ego. Buffers can also allow an addiction to continue. The urge to indulge an addiction usually comes from the instinctive center, while the allowance—the permission—comes from the emotional center. But only the awareness of Pure Being is quick enough to see how they work in tandem.

Why can't chief feature see its own buffers?

Because it resides *within itself.* When you see chief feature objectively, from the outside, you will understand what this means. Although chief feature cannot see its own buffers, each combination of body type and chief feature does develop its own peculiar form of buffers and guilt and expectations. In general, active body types with active features are prone to accusing and blaming others, whereas passive body types with passive features tend more to blame and victimize themselves.

Are the 'I's the same as the ego, or part of the ego?

The 'I's themselves do not have a life of their own. The ego gives them life when it visits their neighborhood. The rest of the time they are like psychological mannequins. Without true conscience we know only the neighborhood we are in when we visit it. All the other neighborhoods cease to exist as if hidden in fog. With conscience, the fog lifts. It gets swept away by the clear consciousness of awareness above the city which sees all the neighborhoods and all that we have done in all the neighborhoods. There is nowhere for the ego to hide. But conscience does not last. The fog rolls back in and our contradictions get hidden again. This is why it is important to honor conscience. The more you do, the more often and more easily the fog will lift.

Is conscience the same as the observer in the mind?

It is not the observer as such. It is a realization. It is a dimension of the recognition of Pure Being. The feeling of being the observer in the mind is like one of the 'I's in the city who goes on a flight in an airplane above the city. Now it can see all the 'I's in all the neighborhoods and understand them in a new way. It thinks of itself as the observer without realizing that it is only an 'I' in an airplane. It is not aware of the sky above it or of the void of space beyond that. The sky, meanwhile, sees the plane flying through it with 'observing I' inside.

Is conscience like the positive side of guilt?

Conscience is a realization inherent in the consciousness of awareness, whereas guilt is a reaction produced by the ego. Guilt is one of the ways the ego twists into a psychological shape to cause problems for itself and to dwell on itself. What the fourth way means by conscience has nothing to do with guilt. Guilt is a substitute for conscience. Conscience means seeing things as they really are without judgment. In the case of the past, conscience is a recognition that awareness was being overrun by identification and the ego. This recognition is meant to 'alert' Pure Being. It only becomes guilt when it is appropriated by the mind as a feeling of 'I' did something wrong, or 'I' could have done it differently, or something bad happened to 'me', or 'I' should be punished or find the right person to blame.

Am I right in saying that Ouspensky called conscience a unifying force?

I don't recall that from Ouspensky, but it could be a matter of interpretation. Conscience does not unify the contradictory parts of our ego. The reason is because we would just have a more or less unified sense of ego. What conscience does is expose contradictions that enable Pure Being to recognize itself above all the different feelings of 'I', and above their shared foundation in the ego. This realization clarifies, and in a sense unifies, Pure Being. The same thing happens with negative emotions. Pure Being realizes itself beyond negative emotions and beyond the sense of 'I' behind them.

Pure Being perceives (recognizes) the truth about yourself and others and the world and this perception gets reflected in the emotional center as conscience. It is a recognition of truth. If you manage not to identify with this feeling of recognition, the energy produced by it will deepen Pure Being. But if you do identity with it, it becomes guilt and reinforces the ego.

But doesn't guilt also shine a light on the truth?

Guilt is a negative emotion that forms *after the fact* in response to what has happened. Conscience is a neutral emotion *in the present* about the truth of what is happening or has happened, and it initially includes a degree of emotional pain that comes with seeing the truth about your imaginary picture of yourself and its actions.

Whereas guilt is a *reaction*, conscience is a *reflection* cast by the light of Pure Being. If you can absorb the 'pang' of conscience when it arises, this allows the light of Pure Being to linger and highlight the truth despite it being painful. The more this happens, the closer conscience comes to the present moment where Pure Being can discern the truth of what you are doing *as you are doing it.* From there, conscience can align with consciousness and become an aspect of Pure Being that sees what you are going to do *before* you do it and trigger an emotional 'alarm' not to do it, say it, or manifest it. In other words, not to fall into identification.

Sometimes I am not sure if it is conscience or guilt that prompts me to want to help others?

This is an interesting observation because it points to how the ego operates behind most of our interactions with people. Most of the time, what prompts the feeling to help or accommodate others is what the fourth way calls *internal* considering, which is a mechanical substitute for conscience. The psychology behind it was described very well by Anthony de Melo who gave three examples. The first is when we want to help or accommodate others because it makes us feel good; doing it reflects well on *our* feeling of self. The second is when we do it because it makes the other person feel good, which reflects well on our sense of self *in relation to* how we are perceived by others; they like us for doing it and that makes 'me' feel good about how I am perceived. The third example is when we do something because we are afraid, if we *don't* do it, that it will reflect badly on our sense of self *and* on how we are perceived by others; that if we don't do it, we are a bad person or they might not like us or they might think poorly of us. This third one often feels like guilt or conscience, but it is just internal considering which means it is based entirely on our view of ourselves *from inside* and our *idea* of how we will be viewed by others.

There is also a fourth scenario that does not involve the ego or leave any trace of the ego. This is when we see from Pure Being what needs to be done and can be done, and we act. That is all. There is no self-reflection or self-reward or self-concern. We are completely *outside* the situation and outside the ego, which is why this is called *external* consideration.

~ ~ ~

Essence and Personality

We too must play our parts on the stage of life, but
we must not identify ourselves with those parts.

Ramana Maharshi

What is the difference between our personality and our essence?

Personality is the shell of socially acquired values, attitudes, preferences, and behavior that stem from the influences of family, culture, religion, education, training. By contrast, essence is your innate human being. It includes your physical traits, body chemistry, artistic and athletic talents, and psychological tendencies. You do not acquire these. You are born with them. Personality, on the other hand, is everything you learn and adopt on top of essence, around essence.

Essence also houses the seed of Pure Being that you see in infants who have no thoughts and no ego. Infants do not force an idea of themselves onto other people and they do not judge anything. Those habits form later as part of the psychological ego and its projections and defense mechanisms as a personality. Before that infants simply look without forcing their looking. They are untainted vehicles through which Pure Being sees the world without identifying with it—without establishing itself as an identity *in relation to* what it sees.

Why is this such an important distinction?

The simple being of essence begins its human journey 'asleep' in the sense that it is unaware of itself, which causes it to get attached to the mind and body. This attachment becomes what is called 'identification' because it leads to the formation of identity as an ego. The awareness of Pure Being in essence attaches to the mind, and the mind uses this attachment to generate a sense of 'I', 'me', and 'mine' which perpetuates itself, in most cases, for the rest of a person's life. In the process, essence gets obscured, may atrophy, and in some cases 'dies' even while the person is still alive. Unbeknownst to itself, the only thing missing in essence is the recognition of itself as the seed of Pure Being.

Is essence more or less the same in everyone?

Generally speaking, half the people you know are positively charged, meaning their essence has a positive charge, while the other half are negatively charged. Neither is better, but those who are negatively charged have a harder time accommodating the negative charge of friction caused by pressure in their lives, whereas positive types experience friction in a more complementary way. For instance, where negative types see pressure as a barrier, positive types often see it as an opportunistic challenge; as something to climb over instead of something they have to go through.

And personality is more of a mask, yes?

Although essence is the purest part of us as a human being, it often dons a mask the same way personality does. But the mask of essence is more transparent. You can see essence in a spontaneous smile, a gentle giggle, a look of surprise, an expression of tenderness. You can also see the serious side of essence in someone who is sitting alone, being quiet, reading unobserved, or suffering. In all these instances an innocence and purity shines through.

What is behind the masks?

Behind the mask of personality is essence, and behind essence is Pure Being. The deepest attribute of what is called essence is simple *being*. It is not an identity, a 'me', or an 'I'. It is Pure Being. The true nature of essence is a mystery, which is why science doesn't know anything about it. This part of our nature gets lumped in with the mind and body, but there is more to it. Much more. What makes it a mystery is that essence is a seed that is planted in the soil of a human with the *possibility* of sprouting as the conscious recognition of Pure Being.

Essence is like perfume inside the bottle of the mind and body. They take on the fragrance of essence which lingers in them, but they are not the perfume itself. Recognizing this brings you to a better understanding about the difference between the mind and body which adopt a personality, and the ethereal nature of essence.

Why do we need these masks?

Because Pure Being cannot manifest *directly* in the human dimension. Even essence, which is the closest thing to Pure Being, is too delicate to hold up under the heavy forces at work in humanity. We need the masks, especially of personality, as a buffer to soften the impact of life. The trouble is that Pure Being identifies with these masks. It presumes that it is the masks and that they are real; that the form of identity they project is 'me'. From an early age we learn to view other people and their masks the same way. Everyone interacts *as the identity of their mask* behind which Pure Being is ignorant of itself as the innocence of *no identity*.

People these days seem more confused than ever about their masks. Is this related?

More people may be having psychological issues now because they are frustrated with their sense of identity and either want to find a stable mask or want to tear the mask off. When they try to, they find another mask and then another because it is not possible to remove masks as long as the awareness of being behind them is identified. But it is possible not to identify with thoughts, emotions, appearance, and behavior. What is happening instead these days is a burgeoning of identity crises associated with mental disorders, which are often *internal* masks, and which are partly due to a lack of understanding about the distinction between essence and personality and their relationship to the ego.

What is the connection between personality and essence and ego?

The ego *is* personality. It develops along with personality. Together they are like the surface of the earth, whereas essence is like the atmosphere, and Pure Being is like outer space. The distinction between earth and atmosphere is clear, whereas the distinction between the atmosphere and space is less clear because at some point the sky simply unfolds into space *as space*.

Can you say more about how the ego develops along with personality?

The physiological aspect of each person's essence includes a predominant tendency *around which* their ego and personality develop. The fourth way calls this tendency 'chief feature' because it colors the entire spectrum of the mind's outlook as well as the reactions and behavior of the body. As your personality develops this tendency becomes exaggerated, more extreme. If you have a chief feature of power, for example, it forms as an ego with a psychological propensity to control that can at times be destructive.

If you have a chief feature of vanity, it forms as an ego with a sense of pride and doubt and self-defensiveness. If you have a chief feature of fear, it forms as an identity of timidity, anxiety, excessive caution, and often obsessive preparedness. These are just general examples of three features. There are more.

Does personality form as a result of identification?

Yes. Identification is the psychological progression that happens when Pure Being is drawn out of itself and drawn into whatever object, person, or interest it becomes *aware of*. In eastern traditions this is called 'attachment', meaning that the awareness of Pure Being attaches to what it becomes aware of. The term 'identification' is meant to emphasize that this attachment produces a sense of identity in the mind and body. When Pure Being is *not* identified, there is a different kind of 'recognition'. There is no sense of 'I'. There is simply *being*.

You said the ego is personality. Is this what the word ego also implies in Buddhism?

What Buddhism and non-dualism call the ego is referred to in the fourth way as imaginary 'I' or the 'imaginary picture' you have of yourself. This is the sense of identity you feel inside. When this identity gets projected into the world as behavior, it is called personality because it is the persona of a mental idea and image of yourself. It is a false persona, which is why the fourth way calls it 'false personality'. In this sense, everyone has imposter syndrome because the masks we wear are not what is behind the masks.

Behind all the masks is the void of Pure Being, but because the ego can never resolve this reality it keeps looking for a presumed real version of itself; a deeper feeling of 'I' that it can 'know' and feel comfortable with, especially in relation to other people. This imaginary 'I' is constantly looking for something solid to displace the inner void of Pure Being, and personality is the result.

Can you give an example of false personality?

A common instance is when we feel irritated by someone else's false personality and then lapse into judgment about them. We (as a feeling of self) perceive the falseness in another person, identify with that perception, and then react to it with judgment. All of this reinforces our ego. The psychological device of judgment also deflects the recognition that the ego we are rebuffing in someone else is somehow symptomatic of our own artificial sense of self.

False personality is a form of acting and re-acting without knowing we are acting, without knowing it is a mask. It is all a projection of the ego for the sake of appearing a certain way to protect our sense of identity. This characteristic of the ego has been the same throughout history. It does not form as a point of identity or operate any differently today than in the past, although it does seem to have more extreme manifestations as evidenced in the proliferation of psychological disorders, mental illnesses, and the need for prescription medications—all of which are now regarded as normal.

When you start noticing false personality in yourself and other people, you can discern its physical as well as psychological 'vibration'. For example, our false personality often causes false personality in other people to vibrate with the same or opposite vibration such that they like or dislike our false personality. Much of the time this is how people relate to each other and respond to each other. Little room is left for the intermingling of essences and a deeper recognition of Pure Being.

So false personality is just another name for the mask of persona we wear?

There is also another kind of mask we can wear when we *know* we are acting. This is what the fourth way calls 'true personality'. It is still a mask but it acts as a representative of something more genuine. It, too, has a vibration but it is more a vibration of integrity. Nevertheless, the mask of true personality can quickly shift into the mask of false personality. We can be true one second and turn false the next. And vice-versa.

Professional actors can imitate many of these masks. The best actors can step behind their own mask, embody the inner character they want to portray, and then project the mask of that character from the inside. The only thing that is not an act and cannot be imitated is Pure

Being in the background void that sees all the masks. But not even actors recognize the significance of this. In most cases *their* ego is simply acting out *another* ego.

Do both the mind and body wear these masks?

The physiology of the mind and of the body are aspects of each person's essence, but the mind and body are also conduits that transmit true personality and false personality. Whereas eastern traditions speak about the mind and body as two entities, the fourth way delineates them in more detail. It describes the body as comprising two centers: the instinctive center, which governs the five senses; and the moving center, which governs all learned movements. The mind, meanwhile, also comprises two centers: the emotional center, which governs our perception of people, human events, suffering, beauty, and creativity; and the intellectual center, which governs the formulation of ideas, concepts, language, logic, and points of view.

All four centers can work in harmony, but this does not always happen. For example, when we are identified, the energy circulating in the centers starts to combust in a way that causes them to become hyper, overwork, overlap, interfere with each other, impede one another, and, most importantly, obscure the recognition of Pure Being.

The four centers are also responsible for generating impulses which the ego takes ownership of as the feeling of 'I'. For instance, the instinctive center generates an impulse of hunger or thirst or weariness which prompts the sense of 'I' am hungry, 'I' am thirsty, 'I' am tired. The same thing happens with impulses in the moving center which manifest psychologically as 'I' need to go now, 'I' am in a hurry, 'I' want to finish this project. Impulses from the intellectual center manifest as 'I' think so, 'I' know, 'I' decided, while impulses from the emotional center manifest as 'I' like, 'I' feel, 'I' disapprove.

Each center also has a positive and a negative half which generate positively and negatively charged impulses respectively. These multiple impulses of *energy* are appropriated as a general sense of *identity* by the ego which we experience as the overarching sense of 'me'.

Beyond all of this is Pure Being which is not an impulse or thought or feeling of identity. The only way to try to describe it is to say that it is a void of being which is always here but without recognizing its *beingness*.

What do the four centers have to do with personality and the masks of personality?

As the fourth way explains, one of the four centers is predominant in each person as their 'center of gravity'. One way to describe it is that everyone naturally leans on and relies on one center more than the others, and their personality develops around it accordingly. If the instinctive center is predominant, a person's interests revolve around concerns about energy, health, appearance, and security. Moving-centered people revolve around activities, projects, accomplishments. Emotionally centered people live for relationships, social turmoil, and ideals of happiness and harmony; while intellectually centered people spend their energy on ideas, theories, data, definitions, logic, and proofs.

People with the same center of gravity 'understand' each other. They also see and react to the world differently than people with other centers of gravity. This is because each center of gravity chews on a different kind of food and is not interested in what others are eating, which partly explains why people do not empathize with one another and why they expect and often require others to be more like them.

What happens to pure awareness? Does it become part of a person's center of gravity?

Center of gravity is something you are born with. But when Pure Being identifies with your center of gravity, your sense of identity—your ego—forms around your center of gravity. Identification is a chemical change that takes place when the awareness of Pure Being attaches itself to the four centers. As this happens, the energy of Pure Being ripples through the four centers and sticks to them as a sense of 'I'. On the other hand, when Pure Being remains consciously aware, it still passes through the centers but without getting stuck as a sense of 'I'.

This seems to run contrary to Gurdjieff's description of the four centers working in harmony?

Gurdjieff was explaining how the four centers are *connected* and how they *can* work in harmony, which is true despite a person's center of gravity. He borrowed from ancient teachings with the image of a carriage, horse, and driver where the carriage and the wheels symbolize the instinctive and moving centers, the horse the emotional center, and the driver the intellectual center. Pure Being is the passenger in the back seat whom neither the carriage, the horse, nor the driver realize is there. The carriage is connected to the horse by a shaft, while the horse is connected to the driver with reins, and sometimes the help of a whip. The driver, however, cannot control the carriage other than by controlling the horse (or by using a handbrake). Sometimes the driver gets distracted. Sometimes the horse is temperamental and stubborn. Sometimes the wheels get out of alignment and cause steering problems. All the while, the carriage needs to be oiled, the horse needs to be fed, and the driver needs to know where he is going.

The passenger in the back is on a temporary ride, and in most cases is having a long nap while dreaming about *being* the driver, the horse, and the carriage. Napping means being identified which affects the entire operation because it sends a current of energy that not only disturbs all the parts but allows their energies to infiltrate one another. This changes when the passenger 'wakes up'. When this happens, the centers stop infiltrating one another. They each perform their own job with their own energy *and* in full tandem. Under the full 'recognition' of the passenger, the whole contraption starts to work with more coordination, cooperation, and unity.

I often feel stuck in my personality at work, but when I go for a walk or spend time at the beach I feel more at ease with myself and things in general.

One reason humans often feel at ease and in tune with nature is because nature is the essence of the earth which resonates with the same frequency as essence. Nature has no ego. It simply is what it is, as it is. It projects the *energy of life* in form but without a mask. This same resonance is reflected in great art, which is why the arts are vital for the essence of humanity. Sadly, though, this is not usually why the arts are taught or studied or valued. The arts are usually regarded as *individual* expressions of creativity. They are not understood as manifestations of being which take place *through* the human form, often without the artist understanding the reality of what is happening and how it happens.

Do you mean that art is an expression of essence?

Art can be expressed *through* essence, but the greatest manifestations of art resonate with the emptiness and stillness of Pure Being. For instance, a great dancer may have an extraordinary talent for movement as part of their essence, but their dancing exhibits more than exquisite speed and coordination. Their movements somehow punctuate stillness. The same is true of great musicians. Behind their dexterous play you can detect the silence behind and out of which the music is emerging. You cannot teach this impalpable aspect of art and music and drama, just as you cannot teach someone to think the way great seers think when they look into the silence of the mind and report back. There is a resonance in their words that transcends words themselves.

Essence is not only captivated by these expressions of art; it is nourished by them and recognizes something familiar in them.

~ ~ ~

The Place of Precious Things

Life on Earth

The Place of Precious Things

Everything you see has its roots
in the unseen world.

Rumi

What is the principle of body types supposed to tell us?

That humans are more than a haphazard unfolding of nature. That we are a direct product of the solar system. That we are not on earth accidentally or just for ourselves. That we are *designed* to transform the universal energy of Pure Being in conscious and unconscious ways.

We are tiny links in an enormous chain that transmits influences throughout the solar system. Each human is also an incubator in which Pure Being *may* realize itself as Pure Being. Seeing ourselves as a body type, chief feature, center of gravity, and ego changes the picture of who and what we are, what humanity is, and how both exist inside the enormous mechanism of the solar system. Most importantly, it points to Pure Being as a different dimension that encompasses and incorporates *everything*.

In other words, the universe as a single whole?

What we call the universe and our *idea* of the universe are not the full picture. Everything is more multidimensional than science can know.

The realm of nature, for example, is not really part of the earth. It is a thin sheath wrapped around the surface of the earth. It functions separately, with a different purpose. This in itself is interesting to realize. We also know very little about the interior globe of the earth, just as we know little about what lies deep beneath the surface of the other planets and the sun.

According to the fourth way, all energy in the universe is moving up and down in a series of 'octaves' (like musical octaves) that are perpetually ascending and descending. Negative emotions are a classic example of a descending octave that starts when Pure Being identifies with the mind and body and collapses into them as 'I'. From there it falls into the form of 'I' getting negative, then in the form of negativity being released verbally, emotionally, instinctively, or physically. The formation, manifestation, and expression of negative emotions are all part of an octave that spirals downward, becoming less and less conscious and more and more dense as it goes. The idea behind not expressing negative emotions is to halt this descent and introduce the possibility of turning the octave around.

The fourth way also proposes the theory that the moon is an embryonic planet resting inside the womb of the earth, that its orbit around the earth *is* this womb, and that the embryo is tied to its mother by an umbilical cord which nurtures it so it can eventually rotate on its own, move beyond its orbit, and mature as an independent planet. The instinctive centers of all living creatures on earth comprise the umbilical cord. When they die their life energy passes to the moon as a magnetic field that serves as ballast for the moon. But there is a particular strand of this umbilical cord designed to carry a finer energy to the moon, and it does this when human beings become psychologically identified and negative. These currents release a negative charge that innervates the moon. When Pure Being gets identified in human form and transforms into negative emotions, this unconscious substance passes to the moon and gets absorbed as a special nutrient for the moon.

Science knows that the moon has a significant effect on the tides, and many hospitals see a surge in accidents during the full moon. Similar pressures exerted on the earth's surface by the moon affect our energy and mood and thoughts in ways that coincide with Eckhart Tolle's description of the pain body. For instance, it is not uncommon to experience a resurgence of the pain body during the full and new moon.

As part of this larger scheme, human beings do not exist independently in the solar system. They are part of the cog of humanity within the film of organic life on earth which links the sun, the planets, the earth, and the moon. The theory is that influences coming from the sun get filtered by the planets before reaching the earth, but the earth has trouble passing these influences on to the moon. So the worlds of nature in general and humanity in particular act as filters for mixing these influences and transmitting them to the moon in a way that the moon can receive and digest them for its growth. The fourth way views the solar system as a living cosmos whose direction of growth and expansion is the moon. And ours is only one moon in one solar system in one galaxy.

In what way is the moon 'growing'?

Also according to the fourth way, humanity filters energy from the sun and planets in different ways. One of the ways is by the charge of energy that gets released through the death of all living things on earth, especially when large-scale wars and cataclysms provide huge infusions of energy for the moon. Another way is by the energy that gets generated daily around the world through identification and the expression of negativity.

And the ego is a link in this chain?

Exactly. None of this filtering and transmission can happen without the psychological device of the ego in billions of humans coming into conflict with one another and creating gargantuan surges of energy which the moon siphons for its growth.

The tether of energy produced by negative emotions requires individual egos as well as the collective egos of countries, cultures, races, and religions. Individuals who do not want to get swept up in this net have to lessen identification and neutralize the ego. In this sense, it is not the ego or the culture or the moon that is the problem. It is the identification with all of them. Pure Being has to stop touching them, indulging in them, becoming them, defending them, and expressing them. When Pure Being 'steps back' and recognizes itself beyond all of them, they defuse and it transforms.

What about the film of nature?

The film includes nature but it is more than just nature, which is why the fourth way calls it organic life on earth. All of it together forms an enormous chamber that is approximately 15 to 20 miles thick, which is miniscule compared to the earth's diameter of about 8,000 miles. Organic life includes the surface of the earth, the oceans, the atmosphere, and four 'kingdoms' of life that emerge in it.

These kingdoms differ in terms of space and mobility. The mineral kingdom lives mostly below the surface and is immobile. The vegetable kingdom lives below as well as on the surface and has limited mobility. The animal kingdom lives primarily above the surface and is fully mobile. The human kingdom lives above the surface and is mobile physically as well as psychologically. Beyond all these kingdoms is the kingdom of Pure Being which is unlimited in terms of space, mobility, and perceptivity.

Even rocks may experience the sensation of their *existence*. Plants seem to experience the same plus the sensation of growth. Animals experience the sensations of both their existence and their growth as well as their sensation of movement. And humans experience all of these plus their psychological movement. But only in human beings is the consciousness of Pure Being capable of recognizing itself.

How are we swept into the net as you described it?

Everything occurring in humanity takes place in physical and psychological realms according to planetary and lunar forces beyond our control. The only thing we can control is identification, which we can do by realizing what identification is and how it subsumes Pure Being.

Changes within the atmosphere of the solar system affect the atmosphere of the earth which in turn affects the atmosphere of our body and minds. For instance, changes of barometer and sunshine immediately influence our physical and mental buoyancy. Similarly, the sun's magnetic field affects us and all of organic life in many unknown ways.

We are essentially small instruments inside larger and larger instruments of a celestial framework. Each human being is like a corpuscle in the organism of organic life on earth which includes the mineral, vegetable, animal, and human kingdoms as well as the oceans and atmosphere. This organism covers the surface of the earth as part of the connective tissue of the solar system. It connects the planets to the earth and the earth to the moon so that influences can circulate through this branch of the solar system.

The function of each human corpuscle is to

receive some of these influences from the planets, transform them a certain way, and transmit them to the moon. To do this, they need a circuit that will keep the influences moving. This circuit is an ego plugged into an instinctive center and wired to a chief feature via the psychological process of identification.

Our skyscrapers and cities and civilizations, astonishing as they are, pale in relation to the larger picture of universal reality. But that is also what makes our life here so remarkable because most of universal creation is just creation, just form. It is not also *knowingly* witnessing creation the way we are capable of doing.

You also said that individuals who don't want to be part of the earth's tether have a choice. Is that right?

It is more a change of movement or direction resulting from self-realization. Nothing can come into existence as form without the source of energy which is Pure Being. This energy is in everything and unifying everything, but in most forms it no longer contains the element of consciousness of itself. The human form is an exception in that it is a vehicle through which Pure

Being can recognize itself. When this happens, Pure Being starts to be sensitive to the substance of itself in other forms of creation. It starts discerning itself as the rudimentary source of creation, and in doing so it slips out of the net.

Yesterday you commented that the mind is like the moon. What were you referring to?

The moon and the mind seem to be based on a similar principle of design. Both are lifeless in themselves. Both depend entirely on 'light' to give them life. Neither of them generates its own light. They reflect light and in the process filter and distort the original light.

It also appears *to us* that the moon is orbiting the earth. But seen from another dimension, it is moving inside the sphere of the earth's influence and orbiting around the sun *with* the earth. In this sense it is inside the earth just as an embryo is inside its mother. The earth in turn resides inside the body of the sun's influence and orbits with it around some point in the galaxy.

In a similar way, although the mind appears to operate on its own, it really exists inside the sphere of Pure Being and 'moves' with and as a result of the awareness of Pure Being.

You also referred to the idea of Brahman breathing in and out, and that this is more than a physical phenomenon.

It is possible to intuit that the whole of creation is inhaling and exhaling in the sense of pure formless being breathing *out into form* while simultaneously breathing back *into its source.* I was saying that this may also explain why some people are interested in spirituality and some are not. The mind cannot comprehend the depth and scope of how everything is tied together in the physical, psychological, and metaphysical forms of what we call the universe.

Can you say more about how the collective egos of races, religions, and countries contribute to the net of energy that captures energy for the moon?

It would be one thing if we tied only ourselves into the knot of negative emotions. But we try to tie other people and their negative emotions into the same knot. When this is extrapolated across cities and countries you have a global humanity in constant conflict. You have an expansive field of negativity on a planetary scale that can impact a small moon. This same field of energy requires a consciousness of Pure Being on a scale beyond itself to transcend and transform it.

Consider the billions of people spanning the surface of the earth and all of them pulsating with a combined charge of negative energy. The fourth way suggests that this is how humanity was designed to be for the purposes of transmitting energy to the moon. But no one thinks about this. Everyone takes their negativity personally and uses it to fight the negativity of other people, which only intensifies the energy of negativity. And almost no one considers how all this energy might be better spent.

Does this include the energy we waste in being busy all the time?

Yes. The compulsion to always be doing something, achieving something, or needing to be stimulated is also connected to us being a cog in the clockwork of the solar system. Our lives are driven by forces much larger than us and the pressure of these forces compels us—meaning the instinctive center and chief feature—to foster a sense of identity through physical activity and psychological compulsion. Pure Being is not subject to these pressures except when it becomes identified, which is the only thing holding it back *from itself.*

When Pure Being recognizes the void of itself, it sees that *all* events and things in the world are precisely the way they are supposed to be and that imagining they can or should be otherwise is a distortion produced by the mind and reinforced by identification.

It helps me to step outside at night and think about the universe all around me.

When you look at the night sky, try not to 'think' about the universe. Just look and notice that you are looking. Do not let your looking get swept away by thoughts. Just *be* here, you noticing the universe, and the universe noticing you noticing it.

~ ~ ~

Human Suffering

A gem is not polished without rubbing,
nor a man perfected without trials.

Chinese proverb

Many teachings talk about becoming free of suffering, but the fourth way is different in this respect. Can you talk about the difference?

What we experience as pressure in our lives is due to something rubbing against the mind and body. In fourth way parlance, the pressure of life rubs against the four centers, chief feature, and the ego. The normal human reaction is to resist this rubbing because it produces a charge of negative friction that can accumulate as tension, stress, and pain. All of these are magnified with real suffering which means large forms of friction that are harder to bear.

The normal response to friction is to throw it off, get rid of it, avoid it. This seems correct from the point of view of us as a person, but it is viewed differently from the perspective of Pure Being because the *energy* of friction can transform the recognition of Pure Being.

How exactly?

Friction produces an electric spark. When you bump your knee or scratch your hand or cannot find your socks, a momentary spark appears which you usually resist right away by getting negative about it and expressing that negativity through one or more of the four centers. The energy of the spark dissipates through your negative reaction. But the same thing can happen and instead of bolstering your sense of 'I' through negativity you can use the spark of friction to heighten the recognition of Pure Being. In simple terms, you can use friction to be more present.

The most powerful sparks of friction come from intense suffering and are the most challenging to transform. But the process of transformation is always the same because Pure Being is always the same.

Can you describe the transformation that happens?

There is a slight shift inside when, during moments of suffering, you realize you are seeing the suffering without being part of it. These are important moments because normally all our attention is going toward our *identity* and what *we* are suffering. Such moments present the possibility for Pure Being to realize itself *as the seeing*. Small and large suffering both contain a certain tonic that can be transformed into Pure Being.

What about strong trauma? Can it be transformed after the fact?

People who have experienced trauma may be drawn to the idea of revisiting their past to heal wounds, although you have to question who the 'I' is that is interested in doing the revisiting, what you are revisiting, and what you hope to achieve. When you examine these questions they all have the same answer which is the ego as a deep-rooted sense of 'I' and 'me'. It seems like it wants resolution which is understandable on the level of the person, but when you look closer you see a further indulgence of the ego in itself. It wants to replay events. It wants to imagine that things could have been different and that it would matter if they had been different. In all of this it wants validation and reinforcement. And it gets them because the past cannot be changed.

What happened in the past does not matter the way we think it does. To the extent that it does matter, the memories of difficult moments will present themselves to Pure Being as they need to without us purposely revisiting them. They will simply appear of their own accord and sting us with the pangs of conscience; not to make us feel guilty or resentful, but to show us that Pure Being had been there at the time yet was unaware of *being* in those moments. It is this realization that we are meant to suffer, not the pain of the past. When this happens, and if we don't identify with it, Pure Being becomes more conscious. But it is not about rectifying anything or blaming anyone or reconstructing our sense of 'I'. It is about seeing more consciously than we saw before.

Trauma also has degrees. It can include difficult mental and emotional experiences as well as physical pain, but in all these cases the main thing is to see how the *response to them* stems from the sense of 'I' as the ego. Try to see this without interfering with it or trying to stop it. It is just a series of images projected in the mind, and you are watching it. Focus on being *the seeing* of Pure Being. Let the memory of pain just be there. And just watch 'I' projecting negative thoughts and emotions about it. See that you as Pure Being are free of both and have always been free of both, even when the trauma occurred.

So the fourth way regards suffering as a tonic?

That is just my expression. And it does not apply to all of what we call suffering. The fourth way teaches that real suffering is necessary as a catalytic force to engender the self-realization and self-transformation of Pure Being. It also teaches that we create unnecessary suffering for ourselves through wrong attitudes about ourselves, about events in the world, and about suffering itself. In the main, we take everything too personally *in relation to* our sense of 'I'. The force of suffering comes and we immediately think 'I' am suffering instead of perceiving that the body and mind are feeling the friction we call suffering.

When Pure Being identifies with suffering it *becomes* the body and mind which are suffering. When it does *not* identify, it transcends the body and mind. The force of suffering is a catalyst that makes this possible. Whereas the body recoils from the force of suffering, Pure Being draws on the energy of suffering as a kind of fermentation of self-recognition.

The freedom from suffering you mentioned earlier means that Pure Being never suffers. It is always free, but it needs the catalyst of suffering to recognize this and to retain this recognition. Pain and suffering can be real for the mind and body, but they are aspects of the physical and psychological realms, not of Pure Being. You can't choose for them to go away, but you can choose not to identify with them and not to indulge the sense of 'I' in them.

The Place of Precious Things

Is acceptance of real suffering a means of transformation?

When there is pain and suffering, accepting the pressure they bring is helpful, but only if it leads to more or less complete non-identification. This is because acceptance is a posture of the mind. It does not come from Pure Being and it does not by itself yield transformation. Transformation happens as a result of Pure Being recognizing itself beyond and not being identified with the pressure, as well as not being identified with the mind's acceptance or rejection of the pressure. Transformation is always beyond.

How does the ego play into our suffering?

The psychological superstructure of 'I' is the linchpin of all our problems and all of our unnecessary suffering. They are based on this and rely on this. What would problems and inconveniences be without the ego as their anchor?

It feels painful somehow to just give up problems and watch the ego dissolve.

The pain of the ego dissipating is not a real pain. It is an imaginary pain of an imaginary identity. The Pure Being watching the dissipation is not feeling any pain. It is like pulling a splinter out of your finger. The splinter does not hurt. Nisargadatta, who owned a retail business, used the analogy that the ego acts as customer to sensations, thoughts, and emotions and to all the pains and pleasures that come with them. He pointed out that without the ego there is no customer. Pure Being just sees all the products on the shelf but does not spend itself on any of them and does not take any of them home.

In much the same way, we don't have to sort out all the turmoil in our emotional world if we understand that Pure Being can step out of it entirely. The truth is that Pure Being is already outside. It is just enamored with the view of you as a person with emotional issues that need sorting out. The recognition of Pure Being exposes the psychological illusion of being that person who feels stuck inside the turmoil.

It's also hard to let go of problems that other people have caused us.

For the ego it is hard. But in reality you can't blame something else for your problems. No person or event is trying to pull you into identification. The magnet of identification has to reverse so that Pure Being recognizes itself and sees the hologram of 'I' who is having problems. Problems resolve themselves from there.

Imagine ten people in a room with the same problem. Exactly the same. Look at them closely and notice how their sense of identity is wrapped up in the issue. Suddenly, one of them undergoes the recognition of Pure Being which pops out and sees their person of 'I' embroiled, not so much in the issue, but in itself as a person having an issue. Pure Being looks around and cannot understand why Pure Being in the other nine people is not realizing the same thing and not seeing that the problem is not the real problem.

Can you say more about just letting the pain of suffering be there without interfering?

The best way to manage suffering is to meet

it without resistance and then absorb it in the void of Pure Being. When you feel pain and pressure, try to notice where they are influencing the body, how the body is reacting, and how this reaction is prompting a secondary reaction in the mind and emotions. As you notice this, notice also that Pure Being itself is not feeling any pain or pressure. Let them be as they are. Align yourself with Pure Being. Give the pain and pressure a chance to quietly resolve into the void.

Suffering has a secret door that opens into the vastness of Pure Being. Instead of closing this door and holding it shut, Pure Being can silently slip through it into the infinite dimension of itself. There is an enormous difference between rejecting suffering and welcoming it—in the sense of allowing it to pass *through* you and cleanse you of illusion.

At the same time, suffering belongs to the mind and body, and rightfully so. It is only when Pure Being attaches itself to suffering that we take it personally as the ego. Only then is there something that wants to protect itself from the suffering, and this something is lodged in the body and mind which are suffering. But Pure Being can use the suffering as a lever against which to back itself out of the ego, out of the mind, and out of the body until it is completely in itself as itself. This is the miracle that suffering brings.

Can meditation help bring this about?

Meditation can help you deal with the pressures of fiction and suffering by calming down the instinctive center's reaction and neutralizing the emotional center's response. But the calming effect of meditation is not necessarily transformational. It is often just a normalizing exercise of the mind and the body. You realize this after meditation calms you down only to find yourself getting wound up again later.

Another way to manage pressure is to be aware of your environment as much as you can. See your person in the room feeling the pressure and experiencing the thoughts and feelings accompanying the pressure. Then see your person in the house, in a city, on a planet experiencing the suffering and reacting to it. But rather than focusing on the sensations and thoughts and feelings, keep expanding as Pure Being.

Does Pure Being ever suffer?

What we call suffering cannot touch Pure Being because Pure Being is not in the mind and body. It is strange that Pure Being doesn't know this. But it has to know itself—it has to recognize itself—before it can resolve suffering.

Our body, mind, and sense of identity may be shaken to their core, but Pure Being always remains intact. This is why suffering is necessary because it is the one force strong enough to shake our identity to the core and dislodge Pure Being from its attachment to that core.

When you look at it from the right angle and unwrap the personal sugar coating around it, suffering is not really suffering. It is a force and a test and an opportunity. As Bodhidharma said, "every suffering is a Buddha seed." Will the seed get crushed? Or will it yield Pure Being?

Is this also true with our self-imposed suffering?

Self-imposed suffering is what the fourth way calls unnecessary or imaginary suffering. It is the result of wanting something we don't have and thinking we need it and deserve it, or of not wanting what is happening to be happening and believing it should not be happening to us. In both cases, there is no real force behind the suffering. It is all psychological, all imaginary, all invented by our sense of identity as the ego. So there is nothing to transform. There is just an illusion to let go of. And when we let go of it there is tremendous relief.

Freedom from real suffering, on the other hand, does not mean that the mind and body will be free from pain and pressure. It means that Pure Being transcends their suffering and in doing so transforms the quality of energy *behind* suffering and *within* suffering.

Can god grace us with transformation during suffering?

People often turn to god when they are desperate and suffering, or when they want to help others who are suffering. But this reaction, no matter how genuine, is happening in their sense of 'I' which is *imagining* god to be a compassionate entity separate from themselves; as something other than Pure Being.

The beautiful truth is that the more difficult your suffering is as a person—as 'I'—the more expansive the transformation of Pure Being will be if you can slip out of the one dimension into the other.

~ ~ ~

Spiritual Teachers

The Place of Precious Things

In truth we are not here.
This is our shadow.

Rumi

The Place of Precious Things

How would you describe what teaching is in the spiritual environment?

It is the same as in an academic environment. In both there is an assumption that a teacher's job is to teach so others can learn. This is true, but as Peter Ouspensky said to a student who complained about coming to a stop in understanding, "To learn more, you have to teach." Ouspensky also described in *In Search of the Miraculous* how he came to new insights by explaining what he understood to others. In other words, teachers often learn ahead of their students when they teach. By teaching others they deepen their own understanding. Their explanations refine the raw material of what they know into deeper currents of Pure Being. In this sense, teaching is about more than just transmission of knowledge. It is about the transformation of being in both the teacher and the student.

Teaching is also a process of elimination that produces a byproduct which serves as fertilizer for the minds of others. This fertilizer comes in a variety of forms such as information, inspiration, and encouragement which may sprout in other people's minds and give rise to Pure Being.

Do you think spiritual teachers have a special role to play?

If you consider that part of humanity is a conduit for inhaling Pure Being back to its source, you can think of spiritual teachers as the lungs of this part of humanity. Teachers in education and industry and elsewhere can likewise be seen as part of a different fabric which facilitates the *exhalation* of Pure Being into manifestation as creation. In both cases, teachers form the leading edge of the wave of whichever direction creation is moving.

Is it necessary to be a teacher?

Spiritual teachers have always been necessary, but it does not mean that it is always necessary to be a teacher. It may be even more demanding to be invisible and give the ego no hold whatsoever in relation to other egos. Being a teacher also carries its own temptations. A teacher has to remain genuine so as not to let the instinctive center and chief feature find their way back into the mask of being a teacher.

Can a teacher enlighten or awaken a student?

The Pure Being emanating from conscious teachers is like an invisible wand that arouses Pure Being in others, especially others in whom awareness is susceptible to being aroused. But no one can generate Pure Being in someone else.

When you hear that a teacher awakened a student, it means that the Pure Being in one person was already highly susceptible to self-realizing when the emanations of Pure Being in the other person resonated nearby.

If it was possible to *directly* awaken Pure Being in someone else, this would go against the universal physics of what conscious self-realization is. It would mean that Pure Being is an object that can be manipulated by something outside itself. The only thing a teacher can manipulate in a student is form, typically the tandem of mind and ego. The teacher will trip up the student's mind, or outwit the mind, or completely stymie the ego—all in an attempt to create an empty space in the mind where the awareness of Pure Being can start to recognize itself as the void. As Nisargadatta said, "In the stillness of the mind I saw myself as I am—unbound."

What do you regard as the temptations of being a teacher?

A pure teacher transmits the influence of being through his or her *form* as a teacher. This form communicates to the form of other human beings in whom the influence of the teacher's Pure Being may or may not arouse the same in themselves. Both teacher and receiver, however, can get 'stuck' in their roles—identified with their person—and remain at that level of relationship. In the end, however, the recognition of Pure Being has nothing to do with a teacher or a student. They are both empty vessels.

Each teacher is a conduit that uses different words, analogies, and insights from their experience which is inevitably colored by their body type, chief feature, and center of gravity, as well as by the spiritual environs in and through which they developed.

How does the being of a teacher touch the being in a student?

True spiritual teachers leave breadcrumbs that are coated with hints of Pure Being. The breadcrumbs have a kind of perfume that enlivens Pure Being in others. But teachers do not leave the trace of Pure Being itself because being itself does not exist in time or space. There is nothing to leave. Many followers, however, do not realize this so they latch onto pictures and stories and fantasies about the *person* of the teacher and the physical role they played on earth. They mistake the husk for the ethereal kernel because they have not yet realized the kernel in themselves.

Do you mean that devotion by itself can be misleading?

Yes. And limiting. We rightly admire figures such as Lao Tzu, Buddha, Maharshi, and others, but whether we know it or not, we are acknowledging the Pure Being that realized itself *through* them. When you lose sight of this, and many people do, you pour devotion from your person into their persons. Meanwhile Pure Being recognizes itself as the same Pure Being, and this yields an emotion far deeper than devotion.

~ ~ ~

The Place of Precious Things

Pure Being

The Place of Precious Things

From this mysterious well
flows everything in existence.

Lao Tzu

The Place of Precious Things

Can you offer a simple description of what Pure Being is?

It is impossible to define what Pure Being is, but one way to pose it to the mind is to say that Pure Being is the void behind who you think and feel you are as a person with a distinct identity. This background of simply *being* is always 'here' like an invisible expanse of presence that encompasses your entire person and life as well as all creation and all lives.

Pure Being is not a self. It is not a tangible phenomenon. Nor is it an entity such as god or some celestial spirit or being. It is simply the pure reality of *being* behind the manifestations of the human body and mind, and behind the sense of 'I' they generate. This is why some ancient teachings describe it as being invisible yet closer than your own retina.

This void of being is both who you really are as being, and who you are not as a human identity. The mind and body still exist and still live, but the feeling of 'I' entrenched in them is not the real thing; it is a psychological substitute and nothing more. The mind and body can exist as just vessels for Pure Being without 'I'.

To the mind, all this seems impossible on the one hand and nonsensical on the other. How can you be an empty nothing and a visible something at the same time? How can you possibly live without an identity? And yet there is a much larger reality encompassing what we see and experience as our life as a person.

Is this what is asleep or are we asleep to it?

In spiritual terms, what is asleep and what awakens is Pure Being. The mind, body, and sense of 'I' do not awaken. Something else sees these phenomena as an illusion of identity. We use terms such as awareness and consciousness and witness, but these are labels. Pure Being recognizes its deeper reality which can at best be interpreted by the mind as a mystery.

Pure Being can be thought of as 'real I' except that it is not an 'I' or a feeling of 'I' in the usual sense. Compared to 'I' it is nothing. It is empty. It is void. This is why it remains a mystery to the mind and such a joy to itself as Pure Being.

And this is true for everyone?

Yes, but most people don't realize that every

few seconds they are poised on a universal threshold where Pure Being can either turn to its source as unmanifest being, or collapse into identification with, and become identity as, the mind and body. Human existence is a hinge between these two dimensions which religions call heaven and hell without most people understanding their inner meaning.

So how do we shift from the one to the other?

The way to go from 'I' to Pure Being is to see 'I' as just an image in the mind. It sounds too simple, but that is all you can and need to do. At that point the door starts to open for the reality of Pure Being to recognize the void of its all-pervasive reality. If the instinctive, moving, intellectual, and emotional centers of the mind and body could grasp the metaphysical dimension of Pure Being, they would be Pure Being. But they cannot. Only Pure Being can recognize itself.

And then? How does the view change?

Everything appears the same from Pure Being

The Place of Precious Things

but it is perceived differently because identification has dissolved and resolved as Pure Being. Things that seemed important are recognized as unimportant or inconsequential. The simplicity of the moment is poetic and sacred in the simplest way. The desires and compulsions of identification give way to the wonder inherent in the void of Pure Being.

You say it's all we need to do, but it doesn't seem that easy or accessible.

Some traditions refer to Pure Being as the 'guest', however Pure Being does not arrive or visit. It is here all along. It just makes its presence known to itself. A slight turn of the bulb and the light comes on to expose the illusion of what *seemed like* identity. A simple approach to Pure Being is to notice as consciously as you can what is in your immediate environment, including what is going on inside the mind and body, and to notice that it is being noticed. This aspect of the awareness of Pure Being cannot be grasped by the mind, and it is not the person that becomes enlightened. It is the light inside the person. But it does not turn on *inside the person* so much as it just recognizes *its own light*. And this recognition happens beyond even the light. You as an identity never gain sight of Pure Being. It gains sight of you.

You have spoken about if before in terms of awareness. How do you understand it now?

Pure Being extends itself through awareness the way the sun extends itself through light. For instance, it extends itself as attention in the instinctive, moving, emotional, and intellectual centers where it takes on the hue of each as is passes through them. But at its core it remains Pure Being. *Inside each beam of awareness you will find the thread of Pure Being if you know how to look.*

But the feeling of 'I' as a person seems to persist, doesn't it?

When you look at a painting you are seeing it from outside the frame. Only when you identify with the canvas do you fall into the frame. This is the same relationship that Pure Being has with our life. As soon as it identifies with our life it falls into a dream of identity as a person in the painting. Imagine yourself inside a landscape painting and thinking you are in a real landscape. Then you realize it is just the painting of a landscape. Then you step out of the frame. Then you leave the gallery.

The universe is the ultimate magic theater. You step out of one frame and find yourself inside another and then another. Pure Being keeps stepping out into deeper dimensions of being. As long as we think we are passing through our life, we are in the dream. When we realize that our life is passing through Pure Being *as a manifestation of Pure Being,* Pure Being has stepped out of the dream.

Is that what Ouspensky was suggesting or hinting at with the idea of divided attention?

The idea of divided attention is a technique that Ouspensky devised after he heard about self-remembering from George Gurdjieff. When Ouspensky tried to observe the outside world or his internal thoughts while 'remembering' himself, he became aware of a division between what he was observing and himself as the observer. The arrow of his attention was pointing in both directions instead of only in the direction of what was being observed. This realization revealed to him a new understanding.

Divided attention can also be called double attention or double awareness because you are aware of two things simultaneously instead of just one. Without self-remembering, you don't exist. The only thing that exists is what you perceive, be it a tree or a thought. With self-remembering, you also 'exist'. You now appear inside the same circle as what you are perceiving. There is also another dimension of self-remembering where Pure Being becomes aware of both you and of the object you are looking at. Pure Being is then *outside the circle* seeing both your person and the object your person is looking at. Ouspensky called this 'real' self-remembering. Divided attention was just the beginning.

Where does it go from there?

Normally when we observe—meaning without self-remembering—as soon as we perceive something, the mind jumps in with associations, and Pure Being identifies with the mind's activity. The result is a conviction that 'I' am having thoughts about what 'I' am seeing. But that conviction happens in the mind due to Pure Being having lost recognition of itself and becoming identified with the mind.

Self-realization or 'recognition' means that Pure Being opens the door of self-remembering, then the door of transforming negative emotions, then the door of transcending suffering. It keeps opening new doors into deeper realms of being. Everything Pure Being encounters, everything it becomes aware of, can be a catalyst as long as it retains recognition as Pure Being. But even then there is no final destination to reach. Pure Being simply plunges deeper and deeper into the source of being which is itself. As it does, the notion of 'I' fades in the expanse. The circumference of Pure Being keeps expanding into larger circles as it keeps popping out of each dimension of itself into higher dimensions of being.

It sounds like a perpetual retreating of the spirit.

Pure Being is not a retreat. It is an expanding embrace of reality and the energy inherent in reality. True reality is the invisible *energy* of Pure Being manifesting as visible *forms* of reality. Pure Being transforms everything because it does not rearrange the past or interfere with the present or impose a future. As Huang Po said, it is beyond triple time. It simply resolves everything as infinite being. This sounds both extreme and hollow to say it this way, but that is how it is.

What can we as a person expect when that happens?

You the person are not transformed. It is Pure Being that transforms by recognizing itself as the surrounding void that *includes* your person. Some people have described this as a sudden and complete transformation. Other people get glimpses of the next higher dimension, then they visit for short periods, then for longer periods, then they move there and from there Pure Being starts recognizing even deeper expansions into the void.

The egoic sense of 'me' may not disappear right away, but the more Pure Being recognizes 'itself', the more the ego loses conviction. The feeling of 'I' is no longer as compelling or as in charge the way it had been.

But the person does change in some way, yes?

To be consciously aware as Pure Being means that before you take a step you are conscious of the fact that the body is going to take a step. But you are not directing the body. Likewise, before you open your mouth to talk or eat or cough, you are aware of it, although you are not directing it. Before you get out bed, before you brush your teeth, before you give a presentation at work, before you make a phone call, you 'know'. And not only before, but during all these activities, Pure Being is there realizing itself as Pure Being seeing your person embodied in human form living the life of a human being. Residing always in the background is the gentle recognition *of the background* and of everything manifesting in front of it and *within it*.

But isn't there then some kind of significance in terms of the individual?

Each human being is an incubator for Pure Being to recognize itself in, and a conduit to realize itself through. It is as though the current of Pure Being is passing through the vital circuit of the human form where it can be switched on to recognize itself, or remain switched off to serve merely as a channel for identification.

Our feeling of 'I' revolves in its own orbit like a mouse on a spinning wheel. Everything relates to 'me' and points to 'me' and concerns 'me'. This is the daily existence of the ego in most people. A good question to ask is, if Pure Being was not magnetized to the ego like this, where would we direct our attention, from what would we derive awareness, to what end would we want and be able to *be?*

To get a sense of Pure Being, envision living life without the feeling of 'I'—without this life being 'my' life and 'my' concerns and 'my' need to control outcomes. There would be just the mystery and joy of existence in which the mind and body take care of themselves, which they do anyway, and where the mind and body experience the full gamut of physical, intellectual, and emotional ups and downs, which they do anyway. Meanwhile, there would be no sense of identity attached to them as they manifest, act, and react. There would be simply Pure Being recognizing the mystery of life in its infinite freshness and variety and depth. It would not have anything to do with you as an individual.

But I imagine that the ego would still try to interfere and reclaim its territory?

The ego can obscure but can never defeat Pure Being because Pure Being can see the ego, whereas the ego cannot see Pure Being. The ego exists as an illusion in the mind. The only problem is when Pure Being identifies with this illusion and imbues it with identity.

Pure Being is far more incredible than the mind's elaborate productions by the ego. Pure Being eventually comes back to recognizing that it sees all the productions and projections of the ego and knows they can survive only if it identifies with them.

When there is no identification, what happens?

Pure Being can expand as greater dimensions such that identity as a person is seen as a tiny dot which eventually vanishes in the distance. Envision yourself in a jet flying above the earth. As the jet gains altitude, it doesn't take long for people, cars, buildings, cities, and even countries to lose distinction and disappear. Seen from a great height, they no longer exist as separate things. The same is true of how Pure Being views our person and life. They disappear as singular objects. This is because when you take identity out of problems and negative emotions, you are left with only psychological objects and energy, and Pure Being.

Do sensations and thoughts still pose a problem?

Sensations, thoughts, and feelings are never the problem. The problem is our sense of identity in them. Pure Being pulls back from them, steps out of the feeling of 'me', and recognizes its own pure perception. To the mind, this recognition seems like a return to the source, yet the source never went away. It simply recognizes that all the energy it had been expending through identification with the mind and body had always belonged to the source.

I am beginning to see what you mean when you say that identification means becoming an identity.

Yes. Identification gives you the feeling of

being someone who has thoughts, and those thoughts take on a sense of legitimacy. The ego and the mind then reinforce each other at the expense of Pure Being recognizing itself as the invisible arena in which the ego and mind are playing themselves out.

So things naturally look very different when we are not identified?

This is interesting. Pure Being sees a grape and an egg and a vegetable differently than the instinctive center sees them. It sees mysteries and marvels of manifestation, not just food. As strange as it may seem to the mind, Pure Being knows that the body eating food is one manifestation of itself consuming another manifestation of itself. In the same way, Pure Being sees words, ideas, language, thoughts, and feelings differently than the mind and ego see them. It sees reflections, hints, and hues, not just definitions, opinions, and conclusions.

Pure Being is always here, but when it is unconscious this produces an anxious mind that gropes for definitions and answers to problems it cannot define but which it feels uneasy about. The uneasiness, however, is a *signal* that Pure

Being is caught up in the notion of 'me'. Meanwhile the mind cannot comprehend that its only problem is that Pure Being is not aware of *being*.

In the simplest terms, though, why is this the case?

The light of our attention is usually on the object being lit rather than on the source of light. As a result, we experience our life as whatever object or event is highlighted in the foreground, when in fact that object is the farthest point removed from the source of light. Imagine light reversing the direction of its beam and shining back into itself. Or imagine a celestial source of light beaming its 'attention' from beyond the galaxy, into the solar system, onto the earth, and onto you. Your entire life would appear as a miniscule point of reflected light. But what if that tiny point turned around, reflected the light back to its source, and rode those beams back to the source?

Is that what Ramana Maharshi was pointing to with the inquiry "Who am I"?

He was pointing to the fact that Pure Being resides beyond the mind's attempt to grasp it. He was providing a mental trampoline for bouncing beyond the limits of the mind where only Pure Being can recognize itself. He also knew that being does not participate in inquiry. It sees the mind using inquiry to point beyond the mind. It also doesn't answer the inquiry. It is simply conscious of existing beyond the mind as the answer that is more than an answer. As the source that is more than the light.

Why does Pure Being get stuck in the mind? And can it choose to be free?

It gets stuck because the *perception* of seeing thoughts gets appropriated as a feeling of 'me' having thoughts which imbues the mind and body with the sense of being a person. And because of our features and center of gravity, we each buy into identity in different forms. Some of us buy into ideas, ideologies, and rules. Others buy into projects, formulas, and solutions.

Others buy into health, diet, and physique. And others buy into the emotional turmoil of people, problems, and the world's dilemmas.

Pure Being is none of these. It encompasses all of them, and it chooses to close its hooks of identity around them or to remain free as Pure Being. But this freedom does not mean a free body or free mind or free life or free world. It means freedom from a sense of identity *in relation to* all these forms. If you pull out the thread of identity, they lose their power of persuasion.

The freedom you want is Pure Being, but you the person cannot have that. Only Pure Being can be free from identification with 'you'. This is possible, but only to the extent that you are not identified. Identification keeps you bound to the mind and body and to their limited perceptions of reality. Pure Being cannot return to full innocence and expansion as long as it is identified.

But doesn't this presence or Pure Being in us want to be free?

Pure Being inherently wants to *be*. It cannot help itself, just as the sun wants to shine and cannot help but beam across the solar system. But

Pure Being does not begin its human adventure this way. It has to recognize itself embodying the adventure. This recognition is the ultimate purpose and meaning of life on earth.

Pure Being also does not change. Its awareness simply expands. For instance, before you are interested in spirituality, you don't realize you are having thoughts. You *are* your thoughts. Then you realize you can observe them. Then you realize that you are the observer and this realization transforms into the consciousness of awareness itself, which in turn transforms into the recognition of Pure Being. The same is true about our perceptions of the world. Pure Being is initially unaware of itself. Then it cognizes that it is aware *of* phenomena. Then it realizes it is Pure Being. Then it recognizes itself as the source of itself. It keeps unfurling into itself.

This self-realization is the process of Pure Being lifting itself out of the mire of identification, unplugging the circuit of the ego, and freeing itself from the illusion of identity. When this happens, the human in which it happens ceases to be a mechanically wired circuit and becomes a conduit for Pure Being. This is a significant transformation that represents a return of Pure Being to its origin of unmanifest being which is ultimate freedom.

It is also true that Pure Being is always already

free if it wants to be. This is the miracle and truth of Pure Being. It chooses to be awake and chooses to be asleep. It is choosing right now, but not in the way the mind chooses where to go or what to wear or what to eat. It is an imperceptible knowingness of choiceness that *becomes* choice. It is the energy of unmanifest being electing to remain pure or to reside in form.

Can "I am Pure Being" be a mantra?

Even "I am Pure Being" is a thought. It is still a reflection of perception in the mind. Pure Being itself never answers the question, "Who am I?" It *is* the answer without identity and without the question of identity. It does not require affirmation. That comes from the mind only.

Do we have to be ripe for enlightenment?

Ripe is a good word. When the apple is ready to fall, it does. Before then it cannot fall even if you whack it with the stick of 'effort'. It is simply not ready. It needs to ripen to where the umbilical stem is no longer needed.

Is ripeness evident in the feeling of love for creation?

The feeling of love, even profound love that includes appreciation and gratitude and awe, is not Pure Being. These emotions are byproducts that resonate in the emotional center as reflections of the awareness of Pure Being. Behind them is a depth that defies comprehension. So even when you feel these delicious emotions, realize that Pure Being is seeing them being felt in the emotional center. There is human love and there is the unconfined, unconditional love of Pure Being. One is a phenomenon. The other is an infinite void in which everything resides, including love.

It sounds so true and simple but I don't see it that way when I am identified.

There are many things we don't see when we are identified, and the main thing we don't see is the reality of Pure Being. We think we are 'I'.

What is there to see?

There is nothing to see. Pure Being is like deep space. It is absent of form and color. Nothing is reflected. Everything is absorbed. It is the faceless face of pure conscious being. Yet it knows itself as Pure Being.

So how does it recognize itself?

Each dimension of Pure Being exists in the context of a higher dimension of itself. As it recognizes each next dimension it expands and realizes itself as that dimension. Self-realization becomes the recognition of self-realization again and again and again as Pure Being merges into infinite depths of being.

And what happens when it falls asleep instead?

When Pure Being falls asleep it hibernates in the den of identity as a person. It is held in check by believing and wanting to believe the imaginary idea you have about yourself as a person which is only an image projected in the mind. It is like having a photograph and saying this is me, this is who I am, and believing it and trying to persuade others to believe it. Everyone then walks around presenting their image and validating each other's image. As this is happening and Pure Being is identified, it perceives thought forms and enters into them at the expense of remaining aware as itself. In the process it derives identity from them and imbues them with an identity they don't really have. In both cases it misconstrues itself as the self having thoughts.

Is that what Narcissus represents?

Narcissus needed to see his reflection and fall in love with it to realize that the reflection was an illusion. In reality, though, the person standing on the river bank enamored with his image was also an illusion.

What is your best advice for us right now?

Keep noticing that you are aware of creation and that you are noticing that you are aware of it, and that you are noticing the noticing. Keep following that trail all the way back as far as you can. And don't rely on other people's descriptions, but don't disregard them either because they might help if you trip over your own feet trying to fathom Pure Being.

Sometimes when I sit here I have the sense that we are all the same person. What do you make of this?

All human beings share Pure Being in common. As a result we share the same underlying sense of 'I' behind identification. The *identity* of 'I' takes on different flavors of culture, race, education, upbringing, and so on, but the *root* underneath all of them has the same distinctness of 'me' which stems from the energy of Pure Being. We somehow sense this but our focus goes toward our differences rather than to the common thread we share. I hope you don't lose the thread of that perception because it is part of a larger weave of seeing all creation as the same thing.

I know what you mean. It is easy for a perception like this to get covered over again.

We are wrapped in multiple layers of identification and they all have to unwrap until Pure Being is left with only Pure Being. It is like all the planets in the solar system shutting down at once and all the light in the solar system instantaneously withdrawing into its source. The body of the solar system is then seen as dead, but the source that had enlivened it with light is more alive than ever.

Is that related to becoming desireless?

In a way, yes. But true desirelessness does not mean the absence of desires in the mind and body. It means no urge of desire in Pure Being itself; no need to move away from Pure Being and into form for purposes of satisfaction, security, or identity.

We see desires one way when we are identified. When we are not identified they look different. The more Pure Being settles into itself, the more it prefers just being, without holding onto anything. We are also so accustomed to yielding to desires that we don't see the alternative which is to open the space between the desires and seeing the desires. The more this space opens, the greater the recognition of Pure Being. What normally happens instead is that Pure Being 'sees' creation and identifies with the forms of creations, which in turn sparks an impulse in the mind and body to satisfy themselves by touching, possessing, and manipulating forms. Pure Being then delves into those impulses without realizing that it is caught up in a sense of identity in the mind and body.

Is there a central key to transformation?

The key is non-identification which is the condition of Pure Being without identity. Pure Being can transform something only by realizing itself outside the thing and by recognizing that the thing inside it is a temporary appearance of energy and form. This includes our entire body, mind, identity, and life as a person. These forms capture all of our attention while Pure Being, as the source of this seeing, resides as the most unsuspecting aspect of life on earth as well as in the solar system and galaxy.

You said once that seeing has to see that it is seeing.

The physical eyes are like a pair of binoculars through which Pure Being is looking without knowing it is behind the binoculars. Awareness focuses the binoculars and looks at things. It even thinks it is looking for itself somewhere 'out there'. The mind jumps in and says, "What is Pure Being, where is it, how can I see it, how will I recognize it when I see it," and so on. All the while Pure Being is right here behind the binoculars. All it has to do is recognize it is *here*.

Is this the self seeing itself?

The real Self is not a self. It is the unmanifest 'stuff' of infinite being which cannot be seen or felt or conceptualized. Even the feeling of being present behind your eyes, which derives from the *influence* of Pure Being, is not Pure Being itself. You know this because the feeling of being present is perceivable whereas Pure Being is not. To *be* yourself means to be Pure Being. It has nothing to do with physical energy or the appearance or behavior as a person.

Pure Being frees itself from your person by

unbending its hooks of identification with the mind and body and the notion of 'I' they have entertained for so long. It is not even that Pure Being disentangles itself. It simply recognizes 'I' as an illusion and this recognition unbends the hooks of identification without which attachments have no choice but to fall away.

What does it really mean to unbend the hooks?

Pure Being unbending its hooks means identification dissolving and the ego losing conviction as an identity. Among other things it means you no longer feel the need to depend on others to reinforce you because you see through the illusion of identity in them, too. As a result you gain empathy for the Pure Being trapped inside them and you treat them accordingly. The expression, "Do unto others as you would have them do unto you" really means "*Be* unto others as you would have them *be* unto you." Imagine if Pure Being in everyone silently honored itself in others before, during, and after all human interactions.

You seem to presume that you are not identified but you still use the word 'I'. Isn't that evidence of the ego?

We have to be attentive when we touch the word 'I' and the concept of 'I'. We have to be conscious of what we are referring to and representing. There is also a deeper dimension to this in the sense that we are so accustomed to the feeling of 'I' that even when 'I' speaks for Pure Being, the mind and body think they understand the void of Pure Being. They think it more or less resembles them in some way. But this is not true at all. Pure Being is a different dimension. It is not solidified as a point of form and identity. That is what the mind does to it when it tries to grasp Pure Being *conceptually*. Meanwhile Pure Being is ungraspable. Knowing this, you can be confident when saying 'I' that you are speaking as a mental courier and nothing more.

But when we say 'I' there is still an ego, isn't there?

Not necessarily. 'I' can also be just an instrument while Pure Being remains egoless. In that case there is no identification and nothing for an identity to establish itself around even as we speak and go about the business of the day.

Do problems still present themselves?

Problems do not appear as problems to Pure Being. They appear that way only to the four centers and the ego they engender when Pure Being identifies with them. When we are not identified, things still happen as they are meant to in the mind and body, as well as in nature and humanity, but they do not become issues that have to be wrestled with. Everything is seen instead as inevitable manifestations of energy and form. Seeing them this way expands the recognition of Pure Being. Yet this 'recognition' does not come from somewhere. It is always here. It is just not in focus. When it recognizes that it *is* here, it comes into focus. Then it keeps meeting itself here and in everything. It simply watches what happens without the impulse to interfere or to control an outcome.

In other words, living in the moment?

Some people think of it as 'living in the moment', but this has to be understood in the right way because Pure Being is not about living *in* the moment or *for* the moment. It is about abiding as the background of Pure Being which perceives the mind and body and moment unfolding inside itself. In this ethereal atmosphere of non-identification there is no place for the ego to take hold. There is no 'I' trying to live in the moment. There is not even the moment. There is simply *being*.

How would you describe the emergence of self-realization as it happens?

Self-realization comes as a result of Pure Being seeing that the person of 'me' living this life is an illusory sense of identity, a projection of a mental image, and that there is emptiness behind the image. Out of this recognition emerges the realization of being the Pure Being that sees this, and the realization that the true nature of this Pure Being can never be understood by the mind that is projecting the image.

Why is it called the third eye?

Because, like the lens of an eye, Pure Being has the properties of being able to see and focus as well as go out of focus. When it identifies it goes out of focus. When it self-realizes it self-focuses and then everything else comes into focus. It is also called third eye because it is associated with the pineal gland which is set slightly back in the forehead between the two physical eyes. One theory states that the pineal gland is a receiver for Pure Being, like a gateway through which perceptions of Pure Being pass to the mind. This Pure Being does not see itself, but unlike an eye it recognizes itself.

Is the third eye also the observer?

In the fourth way the witness is called the observer or observing 'I'. We used to say that you are not what you observe; that you are the observer, and that anything which can be observed is not the observer. This is intended to point the mind toward Pure Being. What happens, however, is that as Pure Being begins to recognize itself perceiving, the mind takes ownership of this perception and says 'I' am the observer. Yet Pure Being eventually recognizes this, too.

Is Pure Being detectable in any physical way?

Not directly. The instinctive center, for example, *emanates* energy that radiates as physical intensity, power, sensuality, charisma, and cunning. By contrast, Pure Being *reflects* effervescence, lucidity, translucence, openness, and ease. It does not impose without. It shines from within. But sometimes you can detect its light.

Is the universe a being unto itself?

If the entire universe posed the question, "Who am I," it would be pointing to the same thing we point to when asking this question. Behind it and beyond it is the same purity and consciousness of being.

Why does it take time to reach Pure Being?

It actually does not take time because Pure Being is always here. It is just that against this backdrop sensations arise and in turn prompt emotions and thoughts. When Pure Being is identified, it mistakes itself as these sensations, feelings, and thoughts and sticks to them, and this formation becomes the ego. As Pure Being begins to recognize this, it naturally unforms as the ego which was just a projection all along, and the ego falls away. This may happen all at once. It may also take time for the ego to fully dissolve, just as it took time for it to solidify. But the time it takes exists in the dimension of the mind and body. In Pure Being there is no time.

Scientists claim to be getting closer and closer to detecting the nature of Pure Being. Do you agree?

Science cannot pinpoint or understand Pure Being for the same reason that it cannot pinpoint and understand light. Both originate from a dimension higher than that of the mind and body and physics. All forms of creation in the known and unknown universe are expressions and manifestations emanating from the limitless pureness of infinite being which recognizes itself as the source of itself and as the manifestation of all forms of creation which spring from it. It all comes from the same source and contains the same life energy, yet this energy *at its source* is invisible, formless, motionless, silent, unfathomable, infinite, and undetectable.

How do you understand the idea that everything is connected?

Every object you see exists inside a larger object, inside another form. Thoughts and perceptions also exist inside larger thoughts and deeper perceptions. The entire universe is worlds within worlds within worlds that are connected as one whole. But the mind cannot think its way to the perception of this reality.

Will everyone awaken at some point?

Some boats are heading out to sea. Some are returning to port. The same may be true about each human being. Perhaps the Pure Being in some people is being exhaled as part of the life force of creation, while in others Pure Being is coming home as part of the great in-breath to its source. Both seem necessary and both would seem to eventually come to the same thing because they *are the same thing.*

Why do you say that we don't need thoughts as much as we think we do?

As Pure Being starts perceiving things directly, without the filter of the mind, it gets farther and farther ahead of the mind's response to what *has been* perceived. As this happens, thoughts mean less and less because they simply can't keep up.

You say that true being can't be fully described or explained, yet you are doing exactly that.

Although Pure Being cannot be grasped or explained by the human mind, the mind can approximate words, images, and analogies within its psychological realm of concepts. But it can never actually touch or 'know' Pure Being. And

Pure Being can never be explained by the mind because it is infinite, which is a reality the mind cannot grasp. Infinite means that Pure Being is visible as manifest forms of life *and* invisible as the unmanifest source of life. As Pure Being, it also recognizes that all manifest forms of life derive from the unmanifest source of itself. It recognizes that these manifest forms lose recognition of their unmanifest source, and that although they remain unerringly united with the whole, they *become* separate by virtue of no longer being cognizant of the whole. The human being is a remarkable exception to this in that it includes the seed—the potential—for Pure Being to undergo 'recognition' *through* the experience of being a human being. Needless to say, this is huge.

So the best the mind can do is describe the indescribable on its own terms?

It sounds futile but, yes, that's all it can do. And it is futile because compared to the mind and body, Pure Being is empty. Nevertheless, around this emptiness the mind assembles a scaffolding of labels, concepts, formulas, teachings, and techniques, all in an attempt to pin down, explain, contain, and approach the void of empty being.

The feeling of 'I' in the mind is also part of the scaffolding. It is as though the mind sets a projector on top of the scaffolding and projects a hologram of 'me' into the void the same way a large spotlight casts its rays into the night sky. From there the mind persuades itself that it's projection is Pure Being. It 'thinks' the hologram is real. And until Pure Being recognizes itself as the void, it also believes it is the hologram being projected inside its emptiness. It identifies with this projection of 'I' and in doing so imbues the mind with a sense of identity.

The so-called death of the ego means the dissolution of the projection of 'I'. This dissolution happens concurrently with the recognition that the void is the void, and that 'I' is just a mental projection.

And all the labels and concepts are also projections in the mind?

That's right. The void of Pure Being can be envisioned as an empty sphere inside the mind *and* as an infinite sphere surrounding the mind and body. In both cases the mind stands next to it and does its best to stick concepts and definitions onto it. But the mind can do this only from its side. It cannot paste concepts and images onto the void itself. It can only paste them *on itself,* inside the boundaries of its own walls.

Where does awareness exist in this picture?

Unmanifest Pure Being is not awareness although it projects awareness the same way the sun projects light. Essence is also a projection of Pure Being. It is the purest *form* of being in human form. Personality is a further manifestation of being. It is a more dense, more coarse, and more restricted form than essence, and more removed from recognition of its relationship to its source. As a result it feels unique unto itself and imagines that it is independent of the universe.

So everything is a manifestation of Pure Being?

Yes. And all these manifestations—all forms of life—are also manifestations of other forms. For example, solar systems are manifestations of the energy of galaxies. They rise out of and reside in the world of galaxies. Likewise, planets are manifestations of the energy and influence of suns, nature is a manifestation of the energy and influence of planets, and buildings and cars and furniture are manifestations of the energy and influence of human beings. The farther removed a manifestation is from its source, the more 'dense' its form is. Nevertheless, *everything* is a manifestation of *the same energy* from the same source.

Just as gold manifests as infinite forms of jewelry and remains gold, and just as sand can be molded into infinite forms of sand art, so Pure Being manifests as infinite forms of energy while remaining itself. It is already and always *here*, and sometimes it recognizes this reality.

What about human beings as manifestations?

Human beings are also a manifestation of the energy and influence of the planets, which is the central idea behind the theory of body types. Yet unlike the rest of nature, human beings embody a finer, more rarefied energy that stems from the sun as well as from the world of galaxies and beyond. This energy resides in the seed of essence as a *potential* of recognition that ties Pure Being *directly* to its source. This is what makes the form of a human being so remarkable, so sacred, and seemingly so rare in the universe.

Can you repeat what you said about body types being a manifestation of the planets?

The idea is that the energy and influence of the planets manifest in a way that steers the physical and psychological forms which we know as the body and mind. According to the fourth way, the planets influence the glands which release hormones that influence your physical shape and your psychology, both of which reflect the nature of the informing planet. People are not independently 'doing' their lives. Their lives depend on and are being driven by the influence of the planets. And the ego is simply a form of artificial intelligence that obscures this reality.

And the body and mind are also manifestations?

Physical sensations are manifestations of energy of the instinctive center; movements are manifestations of energy of the body; thoughts are manifestations of energy of the intellectual center; and emotions are manifestations of energy of the emotional center. Negative emotions are manifestations of energy from all four centers in combination with chief feature and the ego. Negative emotions are the most dense form of psychological matter. They are like a petrification of identity. In this sense, transforming negative emotions is akin to solid rocks transmuting into vapor.

If awareness is aware of forms, how can it also be a form?

Even when it is 'aware of being aware', it is still form, albeit a rarefied form and seemingly the most rarefied form that Pure Being can manifest, which is exactly why it enables the realization of 'awakening'. Pure Being, however, is not aware, nor does it become aware or awaken. It simply *is* and as such it recognizes its 'isness'. This source of Pure Being does not look out. It simply *is*, and this 'isness' radiates awareness.

The Place of Precious Things

I asked you about Brahman earlier. Can you say more about how you understand this concept?

The source of Pure Being breathes out the energy of itself into form and draws form back into itself. Creation is its oxygen. But the human being is unique in that it is a form of energy which also includes the capacity to 'look back' at its unmanifest source, which means Pure Being recognizing itself. The mind and body and person never reach or achieve Pure Being. They are part of the exhalation and they eventually dissolve and resolve into Pure Being which is *here* all along. And the mystery in this equation is the gossamer thread of essence which lies at the thin threshold between human form and Pure Being.

Is Pure Being both identification and non-identification?

Pure Being is pure non-identification where there is no identity, no impulse toward identity, and no need for identity. Just Pure Being. At the other end of the spectrum are the ego and negative emotions which represent full identification, solidified identity, a constant urge for identity, and an insecure need to be recognized. These, too, are manifestations of the *energy* of Pure Being, but they are not Pure Being itself.

And unconditional love?

Unconditional love is the emptiness of the void of being which contains everything and in which everything is 'welcome'. The love of Pure Being, however, does not do anything to anyone or for anyone or for itself for any reason. It simply *is*.

And yet we can't seem to realize this. Is there any one thing in particular that prevents us from realizing it?

One of the most common obfuscations of the recognition of Pure Being is the irritating sense that 'I' am losing out on something else by having to do what 'I' am doing now. This feeling is based on the presumption that being *and* the satisfaction of being lie elsewhere when the reality is that they are always right here.

Are the higher centers which the fourth way talks about characteristics or aspects of Pure Being?

According to the fourth way, the two 'higher centers' are fully operational but dormant due to identification, and that they awaken to the degree that identification diminishes. One way to understand this is that higher centers are like apertures in the mind which open but do not themselves 'awaken'. As they open they allow Pure Being to illuminate the mind and expose the image of the ego. They are gateways to Pure Being. As the energy of Pure Being pours in through them it generates the light of awareness just as the heat of the sun generates light. These apertures of higher centers are kept shut by the impelling force of identification. The more identification dissipates, the more these apertures loosen and open. Intense suffering often enables this to happen which is why some people have glimpses of Pure Being that do not last because higher centers close again once the suffering passes. The same thing can happen under the influence of certain drugs. In both cases, however, the apertures usually don't open all the way or stay open because the individual is not prepared to handle the deluge of energy and perceptions that the light of Pure Being yields.

The fourth way seems to overcomplicate spirituality and the path to enlightenment?

Some people deduce that the fourth way is too abstract, complicated, and cumbersome. They fail to see that, although the fourth way is delivered to and received by the mind, it is really a conveyance from Pure Being for the benefit of Pure Being. It is a transparent blueprint hung in front of the void of reality. As such, it offers one of the most complete concepts of reality possible for the mind to comprehend.

The life of Jesus seems like a more simple expression of transformation. Would you agree?

What is even more interesting than the life of Jesus and the story of Christ is the unknown authors who crafted both in such a way as to transmit the truth about the illusion of the ego and the reality of Pure Being.

You said something earlier about seeing things directly, without labels and concepts. How is it possible to do this?

It is not something you do by trying to do it because that is just the mind playing with its own thoughts. It comes with the recognition of Pure Being. The awareness of Pure Being perceives things without labeling them. It sees beyond names, titles, terms, and conceptual forms. It penetrates and dissolves those outer layers and recognizes the energy inside the form. Everywhere it looks it sees a reflection of Pure Being glancing back at itself.

Some people appear to try to emanate awareness and imitate Pure Being, or at least their idea of Pure Being. How do you explain this?

The instinctive center tries to own the *sensation* of being aware of being aware by looking intently at other people, or by drawing attention to the body's movements, gestures, and facial expressions, or by exuding an aura and air of presence. Pure Being is none of these things. It cannot be comprehended by the ego. The ego is in its way, obscuring it. And you can see this as you described. It is detectable as a projection of identity as awareness, which is just another form of identity and identification in the body and mind. Pure Being is never on display like that even when its light shines through a person.

You say Pure Being is always right here and so close, but it eludes nearly everyone. Don't you find that strange and contradictory?

It is strange in a way, but it is not contradictory because it is designed that way. By its very nature, Pure Being cannot be made obvious. It has to recognize itself itself. There is no other way. As a result, most people don't realize how much 'I' and 'me' occupy the central focus of their life and keep them locked in their sense of identity. They cannot comprehend an existence without the ego as the focal point around which their life revolves. They do not see that this is exactly what stands in the way of the recognition of the Pure Being that surrounds and encompasses everything, including their idea of themselves as 'me'. It is also strange to initially see the truth of this in yourself and in other people.

Does being a good person matter in the long run?

What human beings experience as their 'self' doing things, accomplishing tasks, weighing decisions, making choices, having fun, enduring suffering, succeeding, failing, doing good, and causing harm has nothing to do with the *source* of Pure Being. This too is strange but true.

What is the best course of action then?

Keep being aware and noticing that you are aware until you arrive at a new place of seeing. Just notice that you can notice the feeling of 'me', the sense of 'my' life, 'my' thoughts, 'my' feelings, 'my' accomplishments, 'my' suffering. Notice that something can see all this and recognize that it is seeing it. This is the mystery of Pure Being. It backs away from the feeling of 'I'. Then backs away from the body and mind. Then backs away from the sense of being the observer of all those. Then backs away from the backing away until it *is* the infinite void of Pure Being.

~ ~ ~

Let there be just a tacit understanding
and nothing more.

Huang Po

The Place of Precious Things

The Place of Precious Things

Monterey, California
2022

The Place of Precious Things

www.ingramcontent.com/pod-product-compliance
Lightning Source LLC
Chambersburg PA
CBHW030036100526
44590CB00011B/224